The First Nations of British Columbia

The First Nations of British Columbia: An Anthropological Survey

Robert J. Muckle

UBC Press / Vancouver

Printed in Canada on acid-free paper ∞

ISBN 0-7748-0663-X

Canadian Cataloguing in Publication Data
Muckle, Robert James.
The First Nations of British Columbia

Includes bibliographical references.
ISBN 0-7748-0663-X

1. Indians of North America – British Columbia. 2. Indians of North America – British Columbia – History. I. Title.

E78.B9M82 1998   971.1'00497   C98-910172-X

UBC Press gratefully acknowledges the ongoing support to its publishing program from the Canada Council for the Arts, the British Columbia Arts Council, and the Department of Canadian Heritage of the Government of Canada.

UBC Press
University of British Columbia
6344 Memorial Road
Vancouver, BC V6T 1Z2
(604) 822-5959
Fax: 1-800-668-0821
E-mail: orders@ubcpress.ubc.ca
http://www.ubcpress.ubc.ca

Contents

Maps and Illustrations

Preface

This book is for readers who would like a fundamental knowledge of First Nations people, cultures, and issues in British Columbia. Relatively few books treat the First Nations of the province collectively, and those that do lack the broad scope of topics covered here. Synthesizing information from diverse sources, *The First Nations of British Columbia* defines and describes First Nations of today and provides overviews of their prehistory, traditional lifeways, and change over the past 200 years. It also outlines government relations, significant court cases, negotiations in the 1990s, and some outstanding First Nations issues.

An Anthropological Perspective

Much of the information presented here is based on anthropological research, and brief descriptions of the nature of that research in British Columbia are included. The work is also based on the premise that understanding First Nations issues and initiatives of today depends on a knowledge of the history, diversity, and complexity of those nations. It should be appreciated that this material is based largely on external perception: the information has come primarily from publications written by non-native scholars and government sources.

Major areas of interest in **anthropology** include the study of the **prehistoric** past (**archaeology**) and the study of traditional lifeways (**ethnology**), and these provide the focus of Parts 2 and 3 of the book, respectively. Culture change, particularly identification of the mechanisms and impacts of change over the past few hundred years, is another key area of interest in anthropology and is the central theme of Part 4.

A Note on Classification, Territories, and Spelling

Not everyone will agree with the classification, territories, and spelling used. As outlined in Part 1, the classification of First Nations is problematic for a variety of reasons, and there is no consensus on the distinction of major ethnic groups or the demarcation of traditional territories. Similarly, there is no consensus on the spelling of various First Nations. The classifications, boundaries, and spellings used here tend to reflect recent scholarly research but are subject to debate and change.

Acknowledgments

Thanks to UBC Press. I am particularly indebted to Peter Milroy for seeing a place for this book outside of the classroom, to Jean Wilson for her patience and general guidance, and to Camilla Jenkins for her extraordinary editing abilities. I thank René Gadacz, Rick Blacklaws, and Patricia Shaw for their thorough reviews of the manuscript. I have incorporated some, but not all, of their suggestions. All errors and omissions are mine.

Part 1
First Nations Defined

What Is a First Nation?

In British Columbia there is general agreement that the term **First Nation** refers to a group of people who can trace their ancestry to the populations that occupied the land prior to the arrival of Europeans and Americans in the late eighteenth century. Nomenclature for such groups, however, depends on context. Although they were commonly referred to as 'nations' from the late eighteenth to the early twentieth century, in recent decades they have routinely been referred to as 'Natives,' **'Aboriginals,'** 'Indigenous Peoples,' **'Indians,'** and **'Indian bands.'** 'First Nations' customarily describes groups formerly known as bands (the Squamish Band, for example, becoming the Squamish Nation) as well as affiliations of distinct bands and/or nations (the Sto:lo Nation, for example, comprising more than a dozen separate, smaller nations). In some situations the **community** itself may be referred to as a First Nation.

Proponents of the descriptor 'First Nation' cite several benefits. First, it alleviates the derogatory and primitive connotations often associated with such terms as natives, aboriginals, and indigenous. Second, it corrects the misnomer of 'Indians,' which resulted from the mistaken belief that Christopher Columbus had reached India. Third, it emphasizes that the ancestors of today's First Nations were in the region prior to the arrival of Europeans. The term 'nation' reflects original sovereignty, and its plural, 'nations,' accentuates the multitude of distinct groups.

Although there is an increasing tendency to use 'First Nation,' it has not totally displaced the other terms. 'Aboriginal,' 'Indian,' and 'band' have specific legal meaning – as described in the **Canadian Constitution** and the **Indian Act** – and are still widely used by the provincial and federal governments. Some people with ancestral ties to prehistoric populations in the area see 'First Nation' as another label applied by Euro-Canadian society and reject it, instead describing their groups with names from their own languages or using such terms as 'people,' 'council,' or 'community.'

Two Kinds of First Nations People

There are two broad categories of First Nations people in British Columbia: **registered** (or **status**) Indians, and **non-status Indians**. The terms 'registered' and 'status' are used interchangeably to distinguish a person whose name appears on a register maintained by the federal government. The criteria for being recognized as a registered Indian have been revised several times by the federal government, with eligibility including such things as ancestry, marriage, education, and occupation.

While most registered Indians have ancestral ties with prehistoric populations, biological relationships have not been necessary to achieve 'status.' It has been possible, for example, for a non-Indian man to achieve status by marrying a registered Indian woman. Conversely, a person with clear biological ties to prehistoric populations may not necessarily be 'registered.' Historically, status was lost if a registered Indian woman married a non-Indian man. Status could also be lost if a registered Indian obtained a university education, joined the armed forces, or became a Canadian citizen. Some people who fit the eligibility requirements may simply have been missed during the registration process.

Being registered brings many benefits, especially for those working and living on a **reserve**. Registered Indians do not pay tax on income earned while working on a reserve or sales taxes on goods purchased on a reserve. Other benefits include comprehensive medical coverage and support for housing and education. Housing and money for education is not unlimited, however, and the First Nation usually determines its members' eligibility.

In 1985 the federal government passed **Bill C-31**, which enabled people who had lost their status, and their descendants, to become registered. At the same time, the government legislated that First Nations would be allowed to create and maintain their own 'band list' of members using their own criteria for establishing membership. As a result, it is now possible for registered Indians to have no affiliation with a specific First Nation and for non-status people to have band membership.

Population, Reserves, and Settlements

There are approximately 105,000 status and 75,000 non-status Indians living in British Columbia. These figures account for about 5 percent of the total population of the province and about 17 percent of the total First Nations population of Canada.

About 50 percent of the registered Indian population lives on one of the more than 1,600 reserves in the province. The reserves range in size from less than one to more than

Qtsaya (Sara Tweedie) and Lorelle Brett Snow on a Nuxalk reserve near Bella Coola, 1997. There are over 1,600 reserves in British Columbia. Census data from 1991 indicate that over 35 percent of the provincial aboriginal population is under fifteen years of age, compared to 19 percent of the non-aboriginal population.

18,000 hectares, total about 3,500 square kilometres, and account for less than 0.5 percent of the land in the province. The majority of reserves are uninhabited. Most of those living on a reserve reside in one of about 350 settlements, with an average population between 100 and 200 people. About 15,000 non-registered Indians live on various reserves, most often through lease arrangements with the appropriate First Nation.

Lease arrangements with First Nations have also resulted in many businesses locating on reserves. Many First Nations themselves also operate businesses on reserves. Consequently, reserves support a wide variety of commercial enterprises, ranging from sawmills to shopping centres.

Bands, Ethnic Groups, Tribal Councils, and Other Affiliations

For most registered Indians, the primary unit of administration is the band. As defined by the Indian Act (1989), 'band' means: 'a body of Indians ... for whose use and benefit in common, lands, the legal title to which is vested in Her Majesty, have been set apart.' The governance of most bands follows the Indian Act, which calls for an elected chief and council, with the number of councillors dependent on the number of band members – one councillor for every 100 members, with a minimum of two and a maximum of twelve.

Reserves and most funds from the federal Department of Indian Affairs (also known as Indian and Northern Affairs Canada) destined for the registered Indian population tend to be allocated to bands. The bands are therefore the most direct channel for First Nations people to obtain their benefits and entitlements as registered Indians.

In many cases bands do not reflect past social and political organization. Due to a lack of understanding by Euro-Canadians, some traditional groupings were deemed to be separate bands while in other cases distinct groups have amalgamated to form a single band. In the past the federal government has also arbitrarily declared some bands extinct. New bands have continued to emerge in British Columbia throughout the twentieth century, through either amalgamation or division.

There are many reasons for the changing number and nature of bands. In the nineteenth century the government created the bands largely for its own benefit, making it easier to administer and control the First Nations. The creation of new bands through amalgamation in the twentieth century has also often been for the benefit of government, in the form of administrative efficiency, particularly as First Nations populations were declining. Recent creation of new bands, however, has most often been at the request of First Nations, usually reflecting more traditional groupings or more efficient administration. Section 17(1) of the Indian Act (1989) states:

> The Minister may, whenever he considers it desirable,
> (a) amalgamate bands that, by a vote of a majority of their electors, request to be amalgamated; and
> (b) constitute new bands and establish Band Lists with respect thereto from existing Band Lists, or from the Indian Register, if requested to do so by persons proposing to form the new bands.

Depending on how one defines a nation, there may be as few as ten or more than 200 First Nations in the province. There are about 200 bands based in British Columbia (see Appendix 1) as well as a few bands based in the Yukon who claim part of British Columbia as their traditional territory. For those who believe that a band equates with nation, there are therefore about 200 First Nations in the province.

Historically, bands were commonly divided into ten major groupings: Haida, Tsimshian, Kwakiutl, Nootka, Coast

Salish, Interior Salish, Bella Coola, Athapaskan, Inland Tlingit, and Kutenai. Although many First Nations people and students of First Nations view this system as very simplistic and an inaccurate depiction of ethnic diversity, it remains widely used.

It is now held that there are about thirty or forty major **ethnic groups** among the First Nations of British Columbia today (Map 1, Appendix 2). The criteria for distinguishing the groups include shared territory, language, and **culture.** Most of these ethnic groups have further subdivisions –

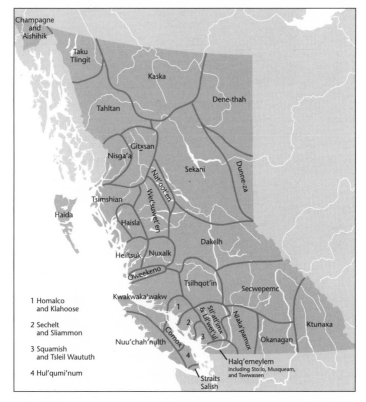

Map 1 First Nations in British Columbia. First Nations are largely self-defined. Identified here are major ethnic groups, based on shared territory, language, and culture. Some are represented today by a single nation; others comprise many smaller nations, sometimes known as bands.

Sel Sil Se Mat (Flo Williams) and her nephew, Gabriel Moody-Thomas, both from the Squamish Nation, 1997. First Nations people often have very strong bonds to their family group and community.

Chester Thomas, 1997. Elders such as Thomas, from Snuneymuxw Village (Nanaimo), are important figures in contemporary First Nations communities. As one of his nieces describes, 'He is our library.'

including nations, community, or family group – to which individuals have a stronger bond. Some scholars, however, prefer to classify First Nations solely by language. This alternative tends to be less problematic than classifying ethnic groups by shared territory and culture as well as language, but it is also subject to debate.

The distinction and mapping of major ethnic groups should be viewed as evolutionary. First Nations people and anthropologists, often in association with each other, are continually working to clarify traditional groupings and territories, but there are many problems: historical records offer contradictory information; Euro-Canadians have often misunderstood language and organization; many First Nations have been known by a variety of names and disagree among themselves; and there are no consistent criteria for distinguishing the groups. As a result, there is no consensus on the number and name of major ethnic groups, let alone territorial boundaries.

Similarly, identification of the specific nations that belong to the larger ethnic groups is problematical, largely because communities have changed, particularly as the boundaries of traditional territories have altered and populations have mixed. It is not unusual for nations to be linked with more than one ethnic group.

About 90 percent of First Nations are affiliated with tribal councils, which are associations of bands formed to deal with administrative, economic, political, or other matters. There are currently about thirty tribal councils in the province. They tend to be regional, and although they are usually formed by nations within a single ethnic group, they may cross ethnic boundaries, as the Carrier-Sekani Tribal Council does, for example.

First Nations people in British Columbia may have many other affiliations, including to organizations that support arts, economic development, health, education, and politics.

Many First Nations have also formed affiliations to negotiate treaties. Some prominent umbrella organizations include the **Assembly of First Nations,** the **First Nations Summit,** the **Union of British Columbia Indian Chiefs,** and the **United Native Nations.**

Suggested Reading

A Traveller's Guide to Aboriginal B.C. (Vancouver: Whitecap Books 1996), by Cheryl Coull, provides a wealth of information about First Nation communities throughout the province and is highly recommended. Readers are also encouraged to read the Indian Act. Lists of First Nations affiliations and organizations are published by the BC Ministry of Aboriginal Affairs in the annual *A Guide to Aboriginal Organizations and Services in British Columbia* (Victoria: Ministry of Aboriginal Affairs 1997).

Part 2

Archaeology and First Peoples

First Nations and Archaeological Perceptions of the Past

The myths of First Nations people in British Columbia often indicate that they have occupied their territories since 'time immemorial' (which can be roughly translated as 'forever') with relatively little change in their traditional lifeways over time. There is considerable variation in details among nations, but origin stories generally follow a common theme. A creator placed people in their territory and then either the creator or other supernatural powers provided values, customs, and languages that have since been maintained.

Although they agree that First Nations people have been in British Columbia a very long time, archaeologists tell a different story about how and when people first came to this part of the world and what cultural changes they subsequently experienced. Basing their conclusions on scientific research, archaeologists state with a high degree of confidence that First Nations people have been in British Columbia for 10,000 years and speculate on earlier migrations through the area.

The Nature of Archaeological Research in British Columbia

Archaeological research began in British Columbia during the late nineteenth century and continued throughout the early twentieth century, with only a handful of professional archaeologists working in the province at any time. Despite the very limited amount of research, a broad outline of the human past in the province was established by the 1960s, including indications of approximately when people first came, what they were doing, and the differences in lifeways in the various regions.

Although refining **culture history** – describing **archaeological sites,** artifacts, and the basic sequence of human events – remains a goal of archaeologists working in the province, the nature of archaeological research has changed significantly over the past few decades. Prior to the 1960s archaeology in

First Nations archaeologist John Jules, 1992. Jules received his degree from the Secwepemc Cultural Education Society/Simon Fraser University program and is currently head of the Archaeology Department of the Kamloops Indian Band.

British Columbia could be characterized as driven by the pursuit of artifacts for museums and the wish to determine an outline of culture history. Archaeological research today focuses not only on what people were doing and when they were doing it but also on why they were doing it and how change occurred.

While pure research interests continue to be important, a significant amount of archaeological research in British Columbia since the 1960s has also been undertaken in the name of **cultural resource management.** Site inventories have been created for specific regions within the province and materials have been collected from sites that have already been or are likely to be destroyed by natural or human processes. During the past few decades much archaeological research has also been undertaken as a result of litigation. Governments and First Nations have contracted archaeologists to undertake research in preparation for court cases involving **aboriginal rights.** Archaeologists have also been contracted

Three Secwepemc archaeologists, 1997: left, Laurie Kennedy (North Thompson); right, Gladys Baptiste (North Thompson); background, Lea McNabb (Skeetchestn). All three graduated from the Secwepemc Cultural Education Society/Simon Fraser University program and are pursuing careers in the field.

by First Nations to assist in the preparation of **treaty** negotiations and to enhance their own understanding of the past for educational purposes. Many First Nations people have pursued careers in archaeology through field work and university training. Collaborative efforts, such as the Secwepemc Cultural Education Society and Simon Fraser University program, provide archaeological training and research benefits to First Nations.

The prehistoric past in British Columbia is protected under provincial and federal legislation. The British Columbia Heritage Conservation Act makes it illegal for anyone without a permit to disturb an archaeological site not on a reserve. Penalties for contravening the act include a fine of up to $50,000 and up to two years in jail for individuals and a fine of up to $1,000,000 for corporations. A person has to meet stringent requirements in order to get a permit: a university degree in archaeology or a related discipline and considerable archaeological field experience. The federal Indian

Act makes it illegal to remove pictographs (rock paintings), petroglyphs (carvings on rock), and carved poles from reserves unless they were specifically manufactured for sale. Penalties for contravening the federal legislation include a fine of up to $200 and up to three months imprisonment. Some First Nations, such as the Sto:lo and Musqueam, have established their own permit system for archaeological research undertaken anywhere in their traditional territories.

The provincial government maintains a record of archaeological sites in the province. The number of sites in the inventory currently sits at about 20,000 and includes a wide diversity of types, including prehistoric villages, rock art, and fishing locations. Shell middens, which are identified on the basis of large quantities of shell deposited as food refuse, are particularly common in coastal areas. Most sites have been recorded by the relatively small number of professional and amateur archaeologists working in the province during the past several decades. Natural processes such as erosion have probably destroyed thousands of sites. Urban development, forestry, mining, dams, road building, and other human activities have probably destroyed thousands more.

Early Migrations through British Columbia

Archaeologists concur that the ancestry of all First Nations of North, Central, and South America lies in Asia and that the route taken from Asia to the Americas was via a land bridge known as **Beringia,** the area surrounding what is now the Bering Strait. Opinion diverges, however, over the timing of the initial migration into the Americas and the route taken from Beringia to what is now the continental United States and areas south of it. Archaeologists are certain of two things: that people have occupied this part of the Americas for at least 12,000 years, and perhaps for 20,000 years or more; and that migrations into these areas involved passing through portions of British Columbia.

While Beringia supported a diverse array of plants and animals, prior to about 11,000 years ago most of what is now Canada was under ice. Exceptions in British Columbia included parts of the outer coast and of the northeastern interior. Some archaeologists speculate that people may have followed the coast south from Beringia; others maintain that an inland route was more likely. The coastal route would have involved short-term occupations of dry land along the coast. The inland route would have followed an ice-free corridor from Beringia through northeastern British Columbia and down the eastern side of the Rocky Mountains into the continental United States. Although most scholars are confident that migrations must have occurred through one or both of these routes between 20,000 and 12,000 years ago, there is no radiocarbon-dated physical evidence of human presence in these areas before about 10,000 years ago. Nevertheless, environmental evidence indicates that both routes were feasible, as plants and animals were sufficiently abundant to support human migrations.

It is likely that sites older than 10,000 years have not been found in British Columbia because they have low archaeological visibility. People migrating along the coast or through the northeastern part of the province would probably not have lived in permanent settlements or created large refuse areas to be identified by archaeologists. Organic preservation decreases the farther back in time one goes, and the relatively small number of people who must have migrated through portions of the province also reduces archaeological visibility. Equally problematic is that sea level, rivers, lakes, and many other landforms have changed significantly over the period, presumably destroying or submerging many sites older than 10,000 years. As well, relatively few archaeologists have focused their research on finding sites in the approximately 10 percent of British Columbia that was not glaciated prior to about 11,000 years ago.

Here to Stay

Environmental and archaeological evidence indicates that by about 10,000 years ago, the glaciers had melted, a wide variety of plants and animals had become established, and people from previously unglaciated portions of North America were settling in British Columbia. It is likely that people came from previously unglaciated areas to the north, south, and southeast of British Columbia, each group bringing its own culture.

Groups occupying British Columbia between 10,000 and 5,000 years ago can be characterized as generalized foragers, typically living in small, nomadic bands and exploiting a wide variety of resources. Archaeological sites reflect a temporary settlement pattern, with no permanent structures, although many sites were revisited many times, probably annually. Fish and sea mammals were important resources to people living in coastal areas but largely insignificant to people of the interior, who relied more heavily on big game. Population density would have been quite low during this period, although people were aware of other groups. The similarity in the remnants of cultures, such as tools, within regions such as the north coast, south coast, southern interior, and northern interior suggests that contact between neighbouring groups occurred.

Settling Down

The cultures of many groups underwent significant change between 5,000 and 3,000 years ago. The unique and sophisticated lifeways exhibited by First Nations of the coast in the late eighteenth and early nineteenth centuries, such as large winter villages, primary dependence on salmon, highly developed stone and plant technologies, complex social organization, and distinctive art can all be traced to this period. Similarly, the development of large winter villages, increasing reliance on salmon, and sophisticated technologies among groups residing in the southern interior can also be traced to this period.

The changes for groups of both the coast and the southern interior were most likely triggered by more efficient salmon processing and storage technologies. The unique, complex, and sophisticated cultures characterizing many First Nations of British Columbia for at least the last 3,000 years are often perceived as being directly related to the ability to harvest salmon in such abundance that it permitted the development of permanent or semi-permanent villages and sophisticated technology. With these changes came larger populations, social stratification, long-distance trade, warfare, heraldic art, and complex ceremonies such as the **potlatch.**

Prominent Sites

Prominent early archaeological sites in the northern interior of British Columbia include Charlie Lake Cave and Mount Edziza. Located in the northeast, near Fort St John, Charlie Lake Cave was first excavated in the early 1980s. The lower levels of the deposit, which consisted of bison bones, tools, and jewellery, were radiocarbon dated to 10,500 years ago, making Charlie Lake Cave the oldest reliably dated site in the province. One of the artifacts found was a fluted point, a type of spear head fairly rare in western Canada but commonly found in sites elsewhere in continental North America and almost always dated to somewhere between 12,000 and 9,000 years ago. Fluted points are usually associated with butchered bison, mammoths, or mastodons. Thus Charlie Lake Cave provides evidence not only of an early occupation but also of considerable interaction and mobility of groups throughout the continent in the early prehistoric period.

Found in many sites in northern British Columbia is a kind of a volcanic rock known as obsidian, which has been traced to the area around Mount Edziza, near Telegraph Creek. Its crystalline structure gives it excellent flaking properties, and obsidian was therefore prized for its use in the manufacture of stone tools. Mount Edziza obsidian has evidently been used throughout northern British Columbia for at least 9,000 years. An archaeological survey of the area in the early 1980s found sites with millions of pieces of obsidian that had been modified by humans. Many sites along the northern and central coastal regions provide evidence of at least several thousand years of occupation. Based on the types of artifacts found there and, in some cases, their location beside prehistoric coastlines, several sites on Haida Gwaii (previously known as the Queen Charlotte Islands) may be older than 10,000 years. Prominent among them is Skoglund's Landing, in which the earliest level consists of some fairly simple stone tools. Unfortunately the site lacks material for accurate dating.

Namu, on the central coast of British Columbia and in the traditional territory of the Heiltsuk, provides a sequence of lifeways spanning close to 10,000 years. Namu is one of the most intensively studied archaeological sites in the province. Excavations during the 1970s, 1980s, and 1990s have provided a wealth of information on coastal prehistory, particularly about subsistence.

Several sites in the 7,000-9,000 year range have been found in the southern interior of the province. Because it contained the oldest human remains in the province, Gore Creek is one of the most significant. Located near Kamloops, the Gore Creek deposit consisted of a young adult male who died in a mudslide. The mud preserved the human skeleton but no artifacts were recovered. The skeleton was radiocarbon dated to a little over 8,000 years, and further testing of the bones revealed that salmon was a minor part of his diet.

Several sites of similar age have been studied in southwestern British Columbia. Relatively few early sites have survived the urbanization of Greater Vancouver but one that has is the Glenrose Cannery Site in Surrey. First excavated in the

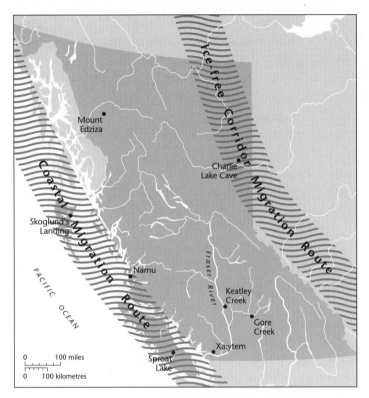

Map 2 Archaeological sites and early migration routes in British Columbia. There are approximately 20,000 recorded archaeological sites in the province.

1970s, the site has provided important information on coastal prehistory over the last 9,000 years. The Milliken site, near Yale on the Fraser River, is another important early site in the region. First excavated in the 1950s, the Milliken site has provided evidence of prehistoric lifeways in the Fraser Canyon as long as 8,000 or more years ago.

One of the most important archaeological sites from the last few thousand years of prehistory in British Columbia is the Keatley Creek site, located near Lillooet. A series of excavations begun in the 1980s has revealed highly complex cultures occupying the southern interior regions for the past

Sproat Lake petroglyphs. These prehistoric rock carvings are located near Port Alberni on Vancouver Island. There are thousands of rock paintings and carvings throughout the province.

few thousand years. With close to 100 houses identified, Keatley Creek is one of the largest prehistoric village sites in western Canada. Variability in the size of houses and the quality of artifacts found within them indicates notable social stratification.

The significance of archaeological sites in British Columbia is customarily assessed according to their value to archaeologists for understanding the prehistoric past. No less important, however, is their value to the public and to First Nations. Rock art often appeals to the public, for example, and in this regard the Sproat Lake petroglyphs on Vancouver Island have substantial merit. Few of the many rock art sites in the province are as accessible. The petroglyphs also have cultural importance in that they are thought to depict mythical creatures and to be the work of a transformer – supernatural creatures common in the mythology of First Nations.

Another site of great significance to First Nations, the public, and archaeology in general is Xa:ytem, also known as the Hatzic Rock Site, near Mission in the Fraser Valley. Like the Sproat Lake petroglyphs, Xa:ytem has easy access and is thought to have been created by a transformer. Excavations at the site during the 1990s have uncovered tens of thousands of artifacts and the remains of houses several thousand years old. The Sto:lo operate an interpretive centre at the site.

Tracing Ancestry

For both scholarly and practical reasons, such as support of aboriginal rights, archaeologists frequently attempt to trace the ancestry of today's First Nations into the prehistoric past. They are confident that direct ancestry for most First Nations can be traced at least 1,000 and in some cases 5,000 or more years into the past. Migrations of groups into territory previously sparsely occupied have been identified, such as movement of a group from the northeastern part of the province into the Nicola Valley in the southern interior several hundred years ago. There is little evidence, however, of large-scale migrations of people displacing pre-existing nations. Boundaries between nations have shifted through time but most nations have probably maintained their core territories for a very long time.

Suggested Reading

B.C. Studies is a quarterly journal that regularly publishes scholarly articles about BC prehistory. Those with an interest in the prehistory of the province are also encouraged to peruse archaeological journals, especially the *Canadian Journal of Archaeology* and *American Antiquity*.

Good general overviews of BC prehistory include Roy Carlson's introductory chapter in *The Pacific Province: A History of British Columbia* (Vancouver: Douglas and McIntyre 1996), edited by Hugh J.M. Johnston, and Knut Fladmark's *British Columbia Prehistory* (Ottawa: National Museums of Canada 1986). Those interested in particular regions or periods may find the following books useful: Donald W. Clark,

Western Subarctic Prehistory (Hull, QC: Canadian Museum of Civilization 1991); Roy Carlson and Luke Dalla Bona, eds. *Early Human Occupation in British Columbia* (Vancouver: UBC Press 1996); R.G. Matson and Gary Coupland, *Prehistory of the Northwest Coast* (New York: Academic Press 1994); and Thomas H. Richards and Michael K. Rousseau, *Late Prehistoric Cultural Horizons on the Canadian Plateau* (Burnaby, BC: SFU Archaeology Press 1987).

A timely collection of articles on the interface of archaeology and First Nations in British Columbia and elsewhere can be found in *At a Crossroads: Archaeology and First Peoples in Canada* (Burnaby, BC: SFU Archaeology Press 1997), edited by George Nicholas and Thomas Andrews.

Part 3
Ethnology in British Columbia

This part discusses the nature of ethnographic research, describes **culture areas,** and summarizes the traditional lifeways of First Nations in British Columbia, as they were when Europeans and Americans arrived in the late eighteenth century. Traditional lifeways are sometimes called 'precolonial,' referring to the time before 1848.

It should be understood and appreciated that although First Nations cultures are for the most part described here in the past tense, many elements of the belief systems, social organization, ceremonialism, and other lifeways have continued to be integral components of First Nation cultures today.

Anthropology and Oral Tradition

The description of traditional lifeways, often referred to as **ethnography,** is one of the basic goals of anthropology. In many places where First Nations did not have written forms of their languages at the time of European contact and where the cultures have undergone significant change since then, such as in British Columbia, anthropologists have relied primarily on **oral traditions** to reconstruct traditional lifeways. They recognize the potential problems in this, including deliberate attempts to deceive, but notwithstanding a few exceptions most information gathered through oral tradition in British Columbia is considered reliable and is supported by archaeological and historical research.

Ethnographic research on the traditional lifeways of First Nations people in British Columbia began in the 1880s and was dominated throughout the late nineteenth and early twentieth centuries by one of the founders and leading figures in North American anthropology, Franz Boas. While living in Germany and studying masks from British Columbia in a museum, Boas became interested in the First Nations of the province. Later he had the opportunity to communicate with a group of Nuxalk who had come to Germany. Boas eventually settled in the United States, where he held various

Nuxalk dancers in costume, 1886. Anthropologist Franz Boas's interest in BC First Nations was stimulated by meeting these dancers in 1886 while they were in Germany.

positions with universities and museums. From there he made many trips to British Columbia to study native lifeways.

As well as providing detailed descriptions of First Nations in British Columbia, the work of Boas had profound implications for the development of North American anthropology in general. Through his work with First Nations in British Columbia, Boas developed the ideas of historical particularism and cultural relativism. Historical particularism states that each society is a product of its own unique history, and cultural relativism asserts that no culture is necessarily better than another. These concepts were contrary to widely held beliefs at the time and became the foundation of North American anthropology. Boas also saw the rapid change that native societies throughout North America were experiencing during the late nineteenth and early twentieth centuries and encouraged his students and others to focus their attention on collecting ethnographic information about these societies.

George and Francine Hunt, 1930. The son of a Tlingit woman and an English man, George Hunt was raised among the Kwakwaka'wakw. His ethnographic research among coastal nations spanned five decades.

Boas also secured funding for large-scale anthropological research projects such as the Jesup North Pacific Expedition, which produced many volumes of ethnographic information on First Nations of British Columbia.

Boas often relied on the research of collaborators such as George Hunt and James Teit. George Hunt was of English-Tlingit ancestry and was raised in a First Nations village. The respect that First Nations people had for Hunt enabled him to collect a vast quantity of information about traditional lifeways, particularly among the Kwakwaka'wakw. His collaboration with Boas lasted forty years. James Teit was of Scottish ancestry but had married and lived among the Nlaka'pamux. His ethnographies of the Nlaka'pamux (Thompson), Secwepemc (Shuswap), Stl'atl'imx (Lillooet), and Okanagan were published under the auspices of the Jesup North Pacific Expedition and are widely referenced.

Other prominent ethnographers of the period included George Dawson, a geologist for the Geological Survey of Canada, who documented First Nations cultures in both the southern interior and northern coastal regions in the late nineteenth century; Charles Hill-Tout, a school teacher who described First Nations cultures on the south coast and in the southern interior in the late nineteenth and early twentieth centuries; Livington Farrand, who worked among the Tsilhqot'in and Heiltsuk in the late nineteenth century; and Marius Barbeau, who worked among the Tsimshian and Haida in the early twentieth century. Prominent ethnographers of First Nations occupying the central and northern interior included Diamond Jenness, who worked primarily among the Sekani and Dakelh in the 1920s.

Ethnographic work has continued throughout the twentieth century, resulting in a multitude of popular and scholarly ethnographies concerned with both traditional and contemporary lifeways of nations throughout the province. Although ethnographic research usually provides an overview of traditional lifeways of specific cultures, some researchers focus on a particular component. Nancy Turner, for example, has published several studies in recent years on the traditional use of plants in First Nations societies of the coast and interior regions.

Musical recordings, paintings, and photographs have also been useful for learning about traditional lifeways. Prominent among the collectors of music were Marius Barbeau and Ida Halpern, who recorded many songs in the early and mid-twentieth century respectively. Though most photographs taken in the late nineteenth and early twentieth centuries were intended to supplement written descriptions, a few individuals made their major contribution to research in the form of sketches, paintings, and photographs. Prominent among them were Paul Kane, an artist whose work gave many anthropologists a more complete understanding of everyday

Haida village of Masset and photographer with his equipment, 1890. Photographers played an important role in documenting First Nations lifeways during the late nineteenth century.

native life, and Edward Curtis, a photographer who produced three volumes of photographs of BC First Nations people.

Information on traditional lifeways has been collected for several reasons: for inherent interest, to preserve knowledge of rapidly changing cultures, and to add to a database that allows research on such basic anthropological goals as understanding the diversity of cultures. Ethnographic work beginning with Boas and continuing into the mid-twentieth century can by and large be characterized as following these objectives.

Although early ethnographers and First Nations worked co-operatively, there is a widespread belief among both natives and non-natives that by collecting and publishing information on traditional lifeways without providing a benefit to the people being studied, researchers have exploited First Nations and their research has in some cases been detrimental. Many native and non-native people have also found the presumption of non-natives to interpret and represent First Nation cultures to be offensive. This view has been applied to anthropological work in British Columbia as well as elsewhere in North America and was articulated in 1969 by

Vine Deloria in his book *Custer Died for Your Sins: An Indian Manifesto:* 'Into each life, it is said, some rain must fall. Some people have bad horoscopes, others take tips on the stock market ... But Indians have been cursed above all people in history. Indians have anthropologists.'

In recent decades First Nations in British Columbia have taken more control over research involving their cultures. Many First Nations now work in partnership with anthropologists, participating in the design and execution of ethnographic research projects and coming to agreements about sharing the results of the research. As with archaeological research, much of the recent research on traditional lifeways has been undertaken in preparation for litigation, treaty negotiations, cultural revitalization, and education.

Traditional Culture Areas of British Columbia

'Culture area' is a core anthropological concept and can be simply defined as a geographic region in which separate societies have similar cultures. Many different nations may, and often do, exist in a single culture area, but taken as a group

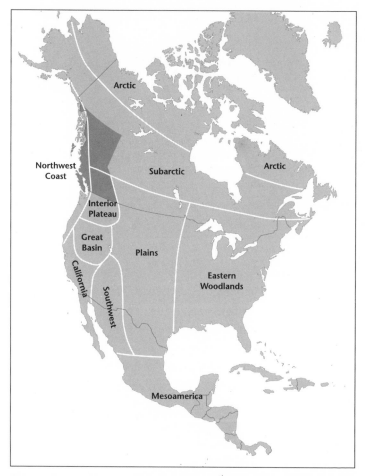

Map 3 Culture areas of North America. First Nations in each culture area shared similar lifeways. The Northwest Coast, Subarctic, and Interior Plateau are each well represented in British Columbia, and the Ktunaxa of southeastern British Columbia have many similarities with Plains cultures.

the lifeways of the nations within a single culture area contrast with the lifeways of nations in other culture areas.

British Columbia includes parts of three of the ten culture areas commonly recognized for the First Nations of North America during the late prehistoric and early historic periods, from the sixteenth to the early nineteenth century: the Northwest Coast, the Interior Plateau, and the Subarctic.

The Northwest Coast encompasses the coastal region extending from Alaska to northern California. The environment is a coastal rainforest with plentiful marine and terrestrial resources. The cultures of the late prehistoric and early historic periods usually had a marine-based economy, complex social and political organization, and sophisticated wood technology and art. Salmon and cedar were important resources, and the characteristic winter dwelling was a plank house. There was a high population density. Major ethnic groups commonly considered as being within the BC portion of the Northwest Coast include the Comox, Gitxsan, Haida, Haisla, Halq'emeylem, Heiltsuk, Homalco, Hul'qumi'num, Klahoose, Kwakwaka'wakw, Nisga'a, Nuu'chah'nulth, Nuxalk, Oweekeno, Sechelt, Sliammon, Squamish, Straits Salish, Tsimshian, and Tsleil Waututh. The Taku Tlingit are sometimes categorized as part of the Northwest Coast culture area and otherwise as part of the Subarctic.

The Interior Plateau includes the southern interior of British Columbia and the interior portion of the Pacific Northwest states – Washington, Oregon, and Idaho. The BC part of the Interior Plateau is also known as the Canadian Plateau. The environment is characterized by its relatively arid climate and diverse landscape. Though marine resources such as salmon were traditionally significant to the economy, the social and political systems were more egalitarian than those of the coast. The characteristic winter dwelling was a pithouse, and the population density was lower than on the coast. Major ethnic groups customarily regarded as being within the BC

Members of McLeod Lake Nation in a cottonwood dugout canoe, c 1912. Both dugout and bark canoes were used among Subarctic people.

Interior Plateau include the Ktunaxa, Nlaka'pamux, Okanagan, Secwepemc, Stl'atl'imx, and Tsilhqot'in. As the boundaries are not well defined, the Dakelh are sometimes judged to be within the Interior Plateau culture area and sometimes within the Subarctic culture area.

The Subarctic includes most of the northern portion of the Canadian provinces. It is bounded by the Arctic on the north, the northern Northwest Coast on the west, and by the Interior Plateau, Plains, and Eastern Woodlands on the south. The environment has forests, numerous lakes, rivers, muskeg, long, cold winters, and relatively short summers. Salmon was an important resource for some groups, but most people depended more heavily on other resources such as moose and caribou. People were more egalitarian and nomadic than those from the Northwest Coast and Interior Plateau. Major ethnic groups of the BC Subarctic include the Dene-thah, Dunne-za, Kaska, Nat'oot'en, Sekani, Tahltan, and Wet'suwet'en, and, in some interpretations, the northern Dakelh.

Languages

None of the languages of the First Nations residing in British Columbia were written or recorded in other ways before the late eighteenth century, so it is not likely that the precise number will ever be known. Given our knowledge of prehistoric cultural diversity, the significant population loss during the early historic period, and the number of languages that have survived to the present, however, it is likely that about fifty were used throughout British Columbia immediately prior to the influx of Europeans and Americans.

Linguists concur that at least eight language families are represented among the First Nations of British Columbia (Table 1). Languages belonging to the same language family may be as similar as Spanish is to French, and languages belonging to different language families may be as different as English is from Cantonese. Although the specific languages belonging to each family are largely mutually unintelligible, there is enough similarity in their cognate vocabulary to

Table 1

First Nations languages of British Columbia, 1998

Language family	Member languages
Algonquian	Cree
Athapaskan	Dakelh, Dene-thah, Dunne-za, Kaska, Nat'oot'en/Wet'suwet'en, Sekani, Tahltan, Tsilhqot'in
Haida	Haida
Ktunaxa	Ktunaxa
Salishan	Halkomelem, Nlaka'pamux, Nuxalk, Okanagan, Sechelt, Secwepemc, Sliammon, Squamish, Stl'atl'imx, Straits Salish
Tsimshian	Coast Tsimshian, Gitxsan/Nisga'a, Southern Tsimshian
Tlingit	Tlingit
Wakashan	Ditidaht, Haisla, Heiltsuk, Kwak'wala, Nuu'chah'nulth

suggest ancestral relationships. That is, the languages in a family have evolved from a common one, usually over at least a few thousand years.

Most linguists agree that about thirty languages native to the First Nations of British Columbia have survived to the present. The problem of reaching consensus on a figure lies primarily in the difficulty of distinguishing dialects from languages, compounded by the relatively few speakers of many languages and the absence of written forms. Languages, for the most part, are deemed to be mutually unintelligible while dialects are deemed to be part of the same language, with minor variations in pronunciation, grammar, and vocabulary.

Haida village of Skidegate, late nineteenth century. The gable roofs, vertical planking, and carved poles are characteristic of winter villages on the north coast.

It is thought that the speakers of different dialects of the same language can communicate effectively whereas speakers of different languages cannot.

Population

Using oral tradition, archaeological research, and historical records, many scholars have attempted to estimate the pre-European population of British Columbia and to identify trends in population density. Estimates of the First Nations population in the mid-eighteenth century range from 80,000 to 500,000 or more, although most anthropologists accept estimates between 200,000 and 300,000. The highest population densities clearly occurred in the Northwest Coast culture area, followed by the Interior Plateau and then the Subarctic area. The coastal region was probably one of the most densely populated areas in North America prior to the arrival of Europeans, and some areas of the coast had higher populations in the past than they do at present.

Settlement Patterns

The Northwest Coast, Interior Plateau, and Subarctic culture areas were each characterized, in part, by settlement patterns. In particular, the type of dwelling and the permanence or impermanence of settlements distinguish the three groups from one another.

Hul'qumi'num village, turn of the century. This village on Vancouver Island illustrates the shed-roof and horizontal planking characteristic of First Nations occupying the south coastal region of British Columbia during the late prehistoric and early historic periods.

A recent chief's pole and house, Masset. The house doubles as a craft shop, selling local Haida art. As in the past, a crest-bearing totem pole outside the house of a hereditary chief among some coastal First Nations confirms their political standing in the community today. Crests in this picture are frog and bear.

Northwest Coast people moved throughout their territory for much of the year but returned to large, permanent villages each winter. The winter village consisted of several large cedar plank houses facing the ocean, each accommodating a different kinship group. Cedar plank houses were characteristic of all Northwest Coast groups but they varied widely in style. One of the most obvious distinctions was the external structure, exemplified by the gable roofs and vertical wall planks of the northern nations, in contrast to the shed-type roofs and horizontal wall planks of the southern nations.

All houses were usually large enough to accommodate several related families, each with its own hearth and living area. Families with the lowest rank occupied the part of the house closest to the entrance, which was nearest the beach. The crest of the kinship group occupying the house was often depicted in paintings and carvings on the exterior and sometimes in the interior of each house. Other common features of the houses included wooden shelves, sleeping platforms, and storage boxes.

Winter village populations on the Northwest Coast ranged between 200 and 1,000 people. They often broke into smaller family groups during the rest of the year, travelling throughout their traditional territory. People frequently constructed temporary shelters from poles, bark, and vegetation. Alternatively, they transported the roof and some wall planks of a winter dwelling, via canoe, from settlement to settlement, simply using the planks to construct a temporary shelter.

In the Interior Plateau people moved throughout their territory to take advantage of the availability of plants and animals. Like the peoples of the coast, they routinely spent winters in permanent villages. Instead of locating these villages near the ocean, as the people of the Northwest Coast did, however, people of the Interior Plateau wintered in major river valleys and built pithouses.

Men in traditional clothing outside a summer lodge near Spences Bridge, early twentieth century. During the non-winter months, Interior peoples often lived in conical structures covered with mats made from rushes or other vegetation. Traditional clothing included garments made from animal hides.

'Pithouse' is the term used by anthropologists to describe a semi-subterranean dwelling typically consisting of a circular depression a few metres deep and approximately six to twelve metres in diameter, although archaeological research indicates that the diameter ranged from four to twenty-two metres during the prehistoric period. After the depression was excavated, a pole framework was erected to support a roof made from poles, bark, tree boughs, and earth. A hole was left in the centre of the roof to serve both as a smoke hole and for access. A slanting log with carved steps was extended from the floor through the hole. Some pithouses also had side entrances. Other common features included a central hearth for cooking and warmth, bark-lined storage pits for food, and floors covered with tree boughs. Pithouses were reused annually. Each was normally occupied by about thirty to forty related individuals, with three or four pithouses in each winter settlement, making an average village population of about 100 to 150.

Ktunaxa men, late 1880s. Like many First Nations leaders, Chief Isadore, centre, had protested against incursions on First Nations territories.

Ktunaxa settlement, turn of the century. The traditional lifeways of the Ktunaxa, including the use of tipis, was more reflective of Plains culture than the cultures of their Interior Plateau neighbours.

During the spring, summer, and autumn Interior Plateau peoples travelled in smaller family groups of between ten and thirty and lived in lodges. The lodges were constructed with a light pole framework covered with materials that depended on circumstances: tree boughs, brush, bark, or rush mats.

These dwellings were not reused, although some of the construction materials were recycled into new lodges.

Although the Ktunaxa were situated on the Interior Plateau, their settlement pattern exemplifies that of nations east of the Rocky Mountains, in the Plains culture area. They lived primarily in villages of tipis constructed of pole frameworks and animal hides, and their seasonal round of activities included crossing the Rockies to hunt buffalo on the Plains.

Unlike the peoples of the Northwest Coast and Interior Plateau, peoples of the Subarctic usually worked year round in relatively small groups, of less than 100, and lived in temporary or portable structures. Their shelters included conical lodges with pole frameworks covered with hides, bark, or brush, and simple lean-to's. During the winter some groups made lodges of poles with moss chinking for insulation.

Diet

First Nations people throughout British Columbia incorporated many types of animals into their diet. Seafood, particularly salmon, was an important component for people living near the coast and along the major rivers. Oolichan, sturgeon, herring, trout, and cod were among the many other types of fish eaten. People living near the coast also ate many species of sea mammals, including seals, porpoises, and whales. Invertebrates such as clams, mussels, cockles, crabs, and urchins were an important form of nourishment for coastal people. Mammals and birds were a substantial part of the diet for most people throughout the province. Deer, mountain goat, marmot, black bear, and beaver were all hunted. Grouse and ducks were among the many types of birds taken for food.

Plants were also significant in the diet of First Nations people in the province. Over 130 species of plants are known to have been used for food, drink, or flavouring. Roots, bulbs, tubers, stems, shoots, buds, leaves, and fruits all provided essential nutrients for most people. Some groups also regularly consumed seeds, nuts, and the inner bark of some trees.

Technology

The First Nations people of British Columbia employed highly sophisticated technologies for their subsistence and material culture. Fishing, hunting, gathering, and cooking were all subsistence activities. Material culture involved the manufacture of practical items and art.

Fish were caught with nets made from natural fibres, spears, baited hooks, and traps. Land animals and birds were hunted with arrows, spears, snares, and traps. Sea mammals were hunted with harpoons. Gathering technology was relatively simple: shellfish and plants were collected into baskets. When necessary, pointed sticks were used to dig through dirt to get at root crops or through sand and gravel for shellfish.

Cooking technology involved roasting food over an open fire, boiling it, or baking it in earth ovens. The technique of boiling food has many variations. The method used by First Nations people of British Columbia is particularly interesting because they often transferred rocks heated in a fire to containers of water, which in turn boiled and cooked the food, instead of placing a pot directly over a fire. Watertight woven baskets, bark baskets, and wooden boxes were all used for this purpose.

People throughout the world use earth ovens to bake foods. There are many variations on the idea of using the heat generated by a fire in a pit to cook foods. The technique in British Columbia involved building a fire in a pit into which meat, fish, shellfish, or edible plants were placed and then covered over with vegetation and earth. Depending on the food, cooking times varied from less than one hour to three days. Sometimes a small hole was left in the covering, through which water was occasionally poured to create a steaming effect.

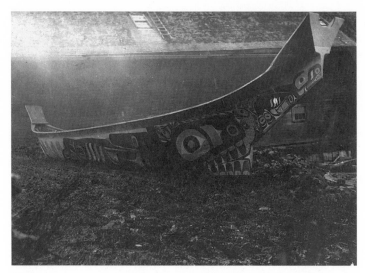

Cedar dugout canoe in a Gitx̲san village, c 1910. Northwest Coast cedar dugout canoes ranged in length from less than five to over twenty metres, could accommodate forty or more people, and were often painted.

Cedar was the most important non-food resource available to people from coastal areas. Not only was cedar the principal component of their houses but it was also used for their canoes and much of their three-dimensional art, such as masks and totem poles. The inner bark of cedar was often used in baskets, and most clothing was made from woven cedar. Cedar canoes ranged from about four to more than twenty metres in length, with a capacity of from one to forty people, plus cargo. They were built from a single log hollowed out with hand tools. Fire was sometimes used to assist in hollowing, and boiling water was often used to steam and soften the wood, which was then stretched and the sides held in place by wooden braces while it cooled.

Cedar was not as readily available to groups in the interior, and they relied more on birch, spruce, and other trees for the manufacture of their canoes and baskets. Interior groups also tended to use more animal skins in the manufacture of their clothing and dwellings than did coastal groups.

Textile manufacture was also known among First Nations, particularly those in coastal regions. Textiles were woven from a variety of plant materials and some animals. Mountain goat hair is known to have been used, and there is speculation that some coastal groups may have bred a small dog specifically for its hair.

Traditional lifeways did not include the manufacture and use of pottery. Most peoples over the past few thousand years with levels of economic and social sophistication similar to those of the First Nations of British Columbia have made pottery. Its absence in the province may be explained by the extremely efficient basketry technology, which produced containers with many of the benefits of pottery and none of the problems. First Nations manufactured baskets that were inexpensive, watertight, and good for storage without being heavy or fragile.

Straits Salish men in goat hair robes, turn of the century. Goat and dog hair were woven into blankets and garments. Clothing was more typically made from cedar.

Social Organization

The social organization of First Nations was complex and diverse. Nations of the Subarctic and Interior Plateau were inclined to be less complex than those of the Northwest Coast. Some interior nations did exhibit social stratification but they were much more egalitarian than coastal nations. Similarly, control of resources by specific individuals or groups within a community occurred among some interior nations but was not as common as among coastal groups.

Social organization among coastal nations was based on kinship, social stratification was rigid, and positions of leadership were hereditary. Descent was determined matrilineally among nations of the north coast and bilaterally among those

Haida woman, 1884. She has a nose ring, labret in her lower lip, and is wearing a Hudson's Bay blanket. Labrets, nose, rings, and other types of jewellery were common among people of the coast, and the quality and quantity indicated the wearer's status.

of the south coast. Material displays of jewellery, clothing, and houses demonstrated high status, as did the giving away of objects. Among some groups, high status was also expressed through a type of cranial shaping. Infants had boards tied to their foreheads for extended periods to elongate the skull.

People of the coast were recognized as belonging to specific **houses** and **clans**. A house was a group of related extended families living together in one of several cedar plank houses making up the winter village, and the leader of the house was the chief, an hereditary position. The house often controlled access to specific resource locations. It was probably the most important social unit for First Nations people living in coastal regions and owned rights to fishing, hunting, and gathering locations, as well as to songs, dances, and stories. It was generally the house, under the direction of the chief, that assigned status, organized subsistence activities, and regulated relations with other groups. Because each house had its own chief, there was no single authority for each village or nation. Although chiefs may have had different status in the village or within the entire nation, decisions affecting the village would have been based on consensus among them.

Clans were groups of related houses from different villages within the territory of the nation. Traditional Nisga'a society, for example, was – and still is – organized into sixty houses, which in turn belong to one of four clans, Raven, Killer Whale, Wolf, and Eagle. Membership was based on a belief that all members descended from a common ancestor, although not all the links were known. Clans were mostly ceremonial units and often depended on symbols – raven, whale, wolf, and eagle – to provide members with solidarity and an easy means of identification. It was taboo to marry someone from within one's own clan.

Anthropologists use the categories of band, tribe, chiefdom, or state to describe the social and political organization of people throughout the world. Specific types of subsistence –

foraging, horticulture, pastoralism, and agriculture – usually correlate with specific types of settlement patterns, economic systems, and other cultural characteristics. Bands, for example, are usually described as having a foraging way of life, fewer than fifty people, and a highly mobile settlement pattern, and as being egalitarian. Yet many of the First Nations of British Columbia, particularly those of the coast, do not neatly fit the criteria. While they may properly be classified as foragers, for example, many of their economic, social, political, and other cultural attributes are much more complex than that normally exhibited by band societies. Rather than use terms such as band, tribe, or chiefdom to describe social and political organization, many anthropologists therefore now describe precolonial First Nations of British Columbia as complex foragers or complex hunter gatherers.

Myths, Spirits, and Shamans
Myths, which are stories about the actions of supernatural beings in the past, are an integral aspect of all cultures and serve many purposes. Myths of the First Nations of British Columbia interpret such natural phenomena as the creation of the earth, the features of the landscape, and the occurrence of specific varieties of plants and animals. Myths also explain the origin of people, differences between ethnic groups, and certain values and customs. For many people, particularly those living in coastal areas, myths are intricately connected with social organization, as status is often tied to the perceived relationship between an individual and a mythological figure. As well, myths are associated with art through their depiction in painting, carving, and performance, and provide education and entertainment.

Myths include characters known as transformers, who could transform themselves and others at will into various animate and inanimate forms. Hundreds of landforms in British Columbia are explained as the work of transformers.

One example is Siwash Rock in Vancouver's Stanley Park; according to myths of the Musqueam and Squamish nations, a man was turned to stone as a permanent reminder of his unselfishness. Because they often accomplished their goals through trickery, some transformers are also known as tricksters. The best known tricksters in the mythology of the coastal and interior nations are Raven and Coyote, respectively.

First Nations people believed in the existence of many types of spirits. As well as recognizing a human spirit, for example, they believed that animals, plants, and other natural phenomena such as rivers, lakes, and mountains had spirits. This belief system, known as animism, is found in nations throughout the world. Guardian spirits were also recognized by many First Nations. They were believed to bestow power during vision quests. Vision quests were usually carried out in solitude by most males and some females after puberty. During the quest, a guardian spirit would manifest itself to the individual and bestow powers that would protect the person and enhance his or her actions.

Shamanism was another integral element of First Nations lifeways. A shaman was an individual, usually a man, with a unique ability to deal with supernatural beings. Shamans could obtain their expertise through birth, training, or a special encounter. They had a variety of responsibilities, including interpreting events, ensuring successful foraging or warring expeditions, and curing people when the cause of illness was unknown or the symptoms were not responding to ordinary treatments. A common diagnosis by a shaman was soul loss – when a person's soul had left the body. As a cure, a shaman could visit the spirit world to retrieve the soul.

Health and Healing

It is thought that First Nations people of British Columbia were well nourished and relatively free from high-mortality epidemic diseases prior to the European influences in North

Nuu'chah'nulth woman shaman, early twentieth century. Shamans were usually, but not always, men. Their tasks including spiritual healing and influencing supernatural powers for success in foraging.

America. Important factors in maintaining good health included the relatively small size of their settlements (at least for much of the year), an hygienic lifestyle, a varied diet, and knowledge of natural medicines.

First Nations people recognized two distinct types of ailments: spiritual and physical. Spiritual ailments were usually treated by shamans. Physical ailments could be treated by any knowledgeable member of the community. They were proficient at mending broken and dislocated limbs using splints and treating infected teeth and gums through cauterization. Treatment of other physical ailments tended

Sweatlodge, early twentieth century. Similar structures are still being built and used by First Nations people for physical and spiritual cleansing.

to depend on knowledge of the healing properties of plants. People in most nations knew of and used at least a few dozen different plants as medicines.

Sweatlodges were an important element of spiritual and physical healing. Accommodating anywhere from one to several people, most sweatlodges were rounded structures with a pole framework overlaid with earth or mats. Much like in a modern-day sauna or steambath, water was poured over hot rocks to create high humidity and heat inside the structure. In addition to their hygienic value, sweatbaths were commonly thought to enhance the effectiveness of plant medicines and to provide spiritual cleansing. Sweatbaths were also used as part of ritual preparations for hunting, fishing, and warring expeditions.

Art

Art was a vital component of all First Nations cultures in British Columbia. Visual arts such as carving, sculpture, and paintings, and performing arts such as storytelling, music, and dance were all practised.

Wooden sculptures in Halq'emeylem cemetery, turn of the century. First Nations of the south coast had fewer totem poles than their northern neigbours, but wooden sculptures such as these were common.

First Nations people throughout British Columbia routinely decorated baskets and other utilitarian objects. Art was most pervasive among coastal peoples, however, where designs were regularly featured on clothing, jewellery, storage boxes, and tools. Coastal cultures are also distinguished by carved and painted masks and wooden sculptures as well as totem, house, and mortuary poles.

The designs of Subarctic and Interior Plateau peoples were conventionally simple. Designs on baskets, for example, were often geometric. They had aesthetic value and may have indicated ownership. Paintings and sculptures were relatively rare.

Designs of Northwest Coast peoples, by contrast, were often complex and highly symbolic. Paintings and low-relief sculpture, in particular, often became abstract. The use of broad black form lines, ovoids, u- and s-forms, splitting, symmetry, space filling, and stylized motifs to depict creatures

Haida man, 1881. He is dressed in ceremonial clothing, has bird down in his hair, and has the crest of his lineage – Grizzly Bear – tattooed in charcoal.

has come to characterize the Northwest Coast art style. Splitting involves creating an image that is mirrored along an axis. Space filling involves covering the entire surface of the painting or sculpture, leaving no space between figures or images. Although Northwest Coast art had aesthetic value, its primary function is thought to have been symbolic. Paintings and sculpture usually reflected kinship. Totem poles, house poles, and mortuary poles depicted lines of descent. Paintings, carvings, tattoos, and clothing often depicted clan affiliation.

The function of pictographs (paintings on rock) and petroglyphs (carvings on rock) throughout the province is often unclear. They are frequently found in places with difficult access and have simple designs. Pictographs are often painted over one another. Some were probably created to record events and identify territory. Much of the art is thought to be the work of shamans attempting to influence supernatural beings or of individuals on vision quests. The simplicity of designs and the practice of painting one pictograph over another suggest that at many rock art sites the process rather than the final product was the most important aspect.

The performing arts of the First Nations included storytelling, dance, and music, frequently as part of social and spiritual events. Myths, legends, and tales were commonly told at feasts and other ceremonies. Although dance and music were sometimes separate performances, they could accompany storytelling. Dancers often wore sophisticated costumes with masks, and instruments included drums made of wood or hide and rattles made from wood, pebbles, and deer or goat hooves. Like many other aspects of culture, some stories, dances, and music of the First Nations peoples were subject to ownership by individuals or kinship groups.

The Potlatch and Other Important Ceremonies

The potlatch ceremony usually took place in the winter. At a potlatch, the host group would announce that an event of

Tahltan people, turn of the century. This photograph shows a shaman flanked by dancers in costume. Even though they are often considered a Subarctic nation, the Tahltan have many similarities to coastal nations, as exemplified by the button blankets and Northwest Coast style of designs on the shaman's clothing. Their organization into clans is also similar to coastal nations.

social significance had occurred or was going to occur. As well as an announcement, the ceremony involved recitation of oral history, feasting, dancing, singing, and the distribution of gifts to the guests. Although some interior nations have held potlatches in the past few hundred years they are associated most closely with nations of the Northwest Coast culture area.

The manifest function of a traditional potlatch was usually to validate a socially meaningful event, such as a person's formal assumption of the role of chief. The recitation of oral history, supported by dancing and singing, led to the announcement. The guests acted as witnesses and their acceptance of gifts indicated acceptance of the announcement. Latent functions of potlatches included the redistribution of wealth through gift giving, the maintenance of alliances, and an opportunity to put on public record all important changes in a group such as births, marriages, deaths, and transfer of rights. Events at potlatches also affirmed an individual's identity and status through the way he or she was treated, educated people, and dramatized cultural values.

Potlatches were not the only major ceremonies of First Nations. People from various communities would gather for diverse reasons. Many First Nations had ceremonies with a large attendance but without all the features of a potlatch. The ceremonies often involved opportunities for socialization, trade, and spiritual displays.

Ceremonialism was also an important component of subsistence activities. It was not uncommon, for example, for First Nations people to undertake ritualistic dancing, singing, and sweatbathing prior to a foraging expedition. A first salmon ceremony, in which the first salmon taken in the season was ritually treated and placed back in the water, was common among Northwest Coast and Interior Plateau nations.

Trade, Slavery, and Warfare

Trade between nations was common. Salmon, nuts, and other types of food were regularly exchanged. Oolichan, caught mostly by nations occupying the central coast, was particularly prized and some of the well-known trading routes into the interior became known as 'grease trails' in reference to the oil rendered from the fish. Manufactured items such as baskets and cedar canoes were often exchanged, as were raw materials such as shell and obsidian. A few locations in the province became major centres where members of several different nations could trade. One was near Lillooet, which was central to several nations of the Interior Plateau and Northwest Coast culture areas.

Slavery was common among the First Nations of British Columbia, particularly in the Northwest Coast and Interior Plateau culture areas. Most slaves were captives of war or the children of captives and accounted for as much as 30 percent of the population of some coastal villages. Among some interior nations a woman and her children might lose their status as slaves if she married one of the local men. Slave status among coastal nations was permanent. Slaves were often traded and sometimes ransomed.

Inter- and intragroup conflict was common among Northwest Coast nations during the late prehistoric and early historic periods and often focused on the capture of slaves or on revenge. Warfare frequently took the form of surprise attacks, and men sometimes wore protective clothing. Taken in the early twentieth century, this photograph illustrates clothing from an earlier era, showing a warrior in a protective rope shirt and woven cedarbark wrap.

Violent conflict was pervasive among groups of the Northwest Coast. Fighting could occur in many contexts, and conflicts between different kinship groups occupying the same winter village or between members of different winter villages of the same nation were not uncommon. Organized war expeditions occurred throughout the Northwest Coast, with the capture of slaves or revenge the primary motivation. Typically a group attacked at dawn, using the element of surprise. Men were often killed and women and children taken captive. War parties ranged from a few warriors to hundreds, and protective clothing and shields were sometimes used. Some villages were fortified.

Suggested Reading

Hugh Brody's *Maps and Dreams: Indians and the British Columbia Frontier* (Vancouver: Douglas and McIntyre 1988) and Terry Glavin's *A Death Feast in Dimlahamid* (Vancouver: New Star Books 1990) are highly recommended. Volumes 6 and 7 of the *Handbook of North American Indians* – June Helm, ed., *Subarctic* (Washington: Smithsonian Institution 1981) and Wayne Suttles, ed., *Northwest Coast* (Washington: Smithsonian Institution 1990) – contain articles on traditional lifeways. Readers are also encouraged to consult ethnographies written by Boas, Teit, and other early ethnographers. Ralph Maud's *A Guide to B.C. Indian Myth and Legend* (Vancouver: Talon Books 1982) includes a list of early ethnographies. Some recent descriptions of First Nations cultures are: Lizette Hall, *The Carrier, My People* (Quesnel, BC: L. Hall 1992); Nisga'a Tribal Council, *Nisga'a: People of the Nass River* (Vancouver: Douglas and McIntyre and Nisga'a Tribal Council 1993); Dorothy Kennedy and Randy Bouchard, *Sliammon Life, Sliammon Lands* (Vancouver: Talon Books 1983). René Gadacz has authored dozens of specific articles, including multimedia, on aspects of BC First Nations ethnography for the *Canadian Encyclopedia Plus* (Toronto: McClelland and Stewart 1996) and the *Canadian World Encyclopedia on CD-Rom* (Toronto: McClelland and Stewart 1998).

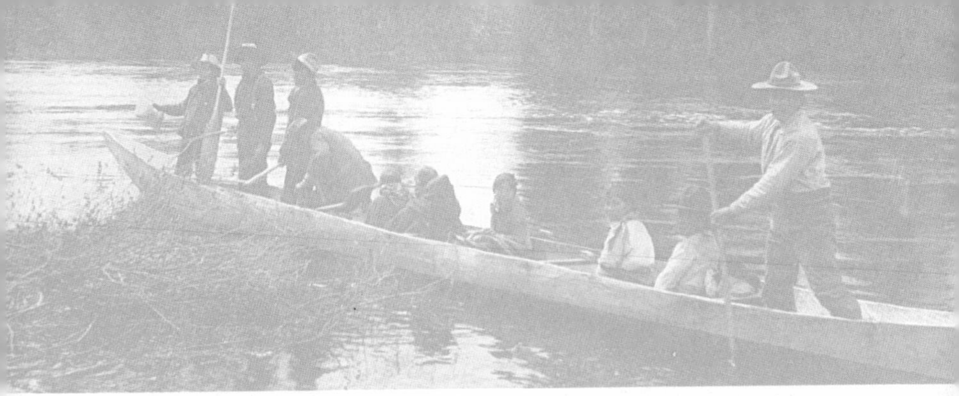

Part 4

Culture Change and Modernization

Beginning with the fur trade in the late eighteenth century, the population, economy, technology, social organization, and many other features of First Nations cultures have been significantly changed. Anthropologists use the term **modernization** to describe the changes that relate to industrial and technological developments. In addition to governments, the major agents of change for First Nations have been fur traders, gold seekers, settlers, and religious orders. This part outlines the impact of these agents. Also described here are colonial, provincial, and federal relations with First Nations, assertions of aboriginal rights, and the current treaty negotiation process, recent initiatives, and some outstanding issues.

Population Loss

From an estimated population of 250,000 or more in the mid-1700s, the population of First Nations people declined to about 100,000 by 1835. By 1885 the population had dropped to 28,000, and by 1929 the population was down to 23,000. This was most likely the lowest figure for at least a few thousand years and may represent a reduction from pre-European times of more than 90 percent. Even using a conservative estimate of 100,000 for the mid-eighteenth-century population, the overall loss was at least 75 percent. Numbers began to increase after 1929.

The major cause of the massive population decline throughout the late eighteenth and nineteenth centuries was diseases carried by Europeans to North America and for which First Nations people had no natural immunity. They also had little access to vaccinations. Deadly diseases included smallpox, tuberculosis, scarlet fever, influenza, and measles. Smallpox was the most devastating of all the diseases, and major epidemics occurred in British Columbia in the late eighteenth century, the late 1830s, and the early 1860s.

Europeans introduced First Nations people to alcohol and firearms, both of which contributed to population loss. In some cases alcohol led to death from accidents and in other cases to social problems and infertility, with consequently fewer births. Although firearms almost certainly increased rates of mortality from conflict, particularly between First Nations, the impact on population was relatively minor compared to that of smallpox and other diseases.

No nation was spared the devastation of significant population loss, and it affected every aspect of First Nations cultures. As leaders, healers, fishers, weavers, carvers, and other specialists died, there was often no one who could take their place. Sometimes cultural knowledge was lost forever. It is likely, for example, that at least several languages have been lost as well as information about the medicinal value of some plants. Dwindling numbers also led to changes in subsistence and settlement patterns. For some groups it became impossible to maintain the traditional round of foraging. Social organization was often thrown into disarray as population loss blurred the once clear relationships between individuals and between groups.

The Impact of the Fur Trade

The first encounters between First Nations and people of European descent occurred in the 1770s. A Spanish ship sailed up and down the coast in 1774, making contact with at least a few First Nations. Shortly after, British and American vessels began an intense period of trading with coastal nations. By the early nineteenth century the land-based fur trade was established with interior nations.

Anthropologists and historians believe that the First Nations were willing participants in the fur trade and there appears to have been intense competition among the nations for access to European and American traders. Not all First Nations people got along with the traders, however, and although rare, violent confrontation did occur, sometimes resulting in death on either side.

Their relationship with First Nations was a business for the fur traders. Their primary objective was to obtain furs for the least possible cost, and there is no reliable evidence that they had any deliberate plan to bring epidemics to the people or to change their cultures. Inadvertently, however, the traders did cause massive changes in traditional lifeways – in material culture, subsistence, and settlement patterns. Many new items of trade were introduced by Europeans and Americans, including metal tools and wool blankets. Metal carving tools greatly enhanced woodworking, and metal pots and kettles made cooking much easier. Subsistence activities were altered to incorporate the desire for fur. More hunting and trapping of fur-bearing animals such as the otter occurred at the expense of other traditional foraging activities. By acting as brokers or intermediaries in the fur trade some groups became less nomadic, and many First Nations started to settle near the trading posts.

The fur trade also altered relationships between nations and between individuals. Some nations developed more power than formerly because their strategic location or influence with the traders enabled them to control trade. Leaders of some nations were able to strengthen their positions and accumulate more wealth by serving as primary negotiators for particular groups.

Traditional lifeways also changed as new markets were created for arts and crafts. Shortly after trade began in the eighteenth century, for example, traders began to seek arts and crafts as well as furs, and some individuals responded by specializing in the creation of arts and crafts for trade. Some people believe that the florescence of First Nations art only occurred as a result of the introduction of metal tools for carving and a market for the art in Europe and elsewhere.

The Impact of the Gold Rushes

A few gold seekers from the United States arrived on the north coast and southern interior regions of the province in the early and mid-1850s but were forcibly driven away by First Nations. The sheer numbers of gold seekers eventually became too great for First Nations to control, however, and it was not long before their impact was felt.

Major gold rushes in 1858 along the Fraser and Thompson rivers, in the 1860s in the Cariboo, and in the 1870s in the north brought about 30,000 gold seekers into the province, significantly altering fish habitat, contributing to changes in First Nations economic activities, and modifying the relationship between First Nations and people of European descent. Unlike fur traders, who depended on the First Nations for their supply of furs, most gold seekers had no need or wish to accommodate First Nations. They were not interested in creating or maintaining long-term relationships with First Nations peoples. As well, many of the gold seekers came directly from the gold rushes of California, where there had been poor relations and violence with First Nations. Many

Gold miners along the Thompson River. Many First Nations people, such as those depicted here, joined the gold rushes of the late nineteenth century.

brought an attitude of superiority into British Columbia, and there are numerous reports of conflicts between the gold seekers and First Nations.

The gold seekers also affected the economic organization of First Nations. First Nations people understood the value of gold, and many became gold seekers themselves. Others gave up their traditional subsistence activities in order to work for wages by providing services to the gold seekers. Many First Nations people traditionally dependent on salmon had to alter their diet because the amount of fish available to them was reduced. Many of the salmon were being taken by and for gold seekers before First Nations people had a chance to catch them. In other cases spawning areas were destroyed by mining activities.

The Impact of Non-Native Settlement

Although there were some earlier attempts at settlement, non-native people did not begin settling in British Columbia in significant numbers until 1858. Some came directly from Britain and elsewhere to establish homesteads; others simply decided to stay after the gold rushes.

Possibly because of the common belief that the First Nations people were doomed to extinction anyway, the settlers did not have a deliberate plan to alter First Nations lifeways. First Nations people were seen primarily as a hindrance, and the major conflicts between First Nations and settlers occurred over land. Like the gold seekers however, the settlers did come with an attitude of superiority.

Backed by the colonial administration, settlers were able to take control of much of the traditional territory of First Nations. Consequently, many First Nations people were unable to carry out their traditional subsistence activities. In order to support themselves and their families many had to leave their villages to look for work in the larger towns created by colonial settlement. This often led to the breakdown of traditional social relations and increased the dependence of First Nations people on settlers.

Missionaries and Residential Schools

Although the history of missionaries in British Columbia extends back into the late eighteenth century, their impact on First Nations was negligible until the late nineteenth century. A First Nations perspective on the introduction of Christianity, particularly the impact of missionary Alfred Hall, is described by Gloria Cranmer Webster in 'From Colonization to Repatriation':

> The introduction of Christianity must have been a confusing time for our people. At the same time missionaries like Hall were preaching, 'Thou shalt not steal,' settlers were helping themselves to large tracts of land ... While Hall was telling the people that, 'It is better to give than to receive,' he was also telling them that lavish gift-giving at potlatches was sinful and heathenish. With all the mixed messages the missionaries were giving the local people, it is no wonder that there were few converts. People had difficulty making sense of it all (p. 29).

It is clear, however, that by the early twentieth century many First Nations people had been converted to Christianity. As anthropologist Wilson Duff notes in *The Indian History of British Columbia,* 'By 1904, 90 per cent of the Indians of the Province were nominally Christian' (p. 87). One explanation is that significant population loss and severe disruptions to traditional lifeways during the nineteenth century prompted many First Nations people to follow missionary teachings. During the initial fur trade period, conditions for most First Nations people had stayed more or less the same or improved slightly. As the impact of the gold seekers and settlers became felt, however, living conditions deteriorated and many First Nations people became disillusioned. They may have begun to accept Christianity to explain or to cope with the economic, social, and political domination that they were experiencing.

Unlike the fur traders, gold seekers, and settlers, missionaries had deliberate plans to change the traditional lifeways of First Nations people. Their intent was to alter First Nations culture completely, encouraging agrarian settlement and abandonment of traditional ceremonies and beliefs.

One well-known missionary, William Duncan, went so far as to set up a new Tsimshian community at Metlakatla in the 1860s. For its nearly 1,000 residents he established a set of rules forbidding such traditional cultural elements as shamanism and potlatching and made mandatory such practices as religious instruction and payment of taxes. In his attempt to get First Nations people away from what he considered bad influences and to assimilate them into Euro-Canadian society,

Metlakatla, 1880s. This community was established among the Tsimshian in the 1860s by a missionary, William Duncan, with a view to assimilating First Nations people into Euro-Canadian society.

Duncan was doing what later church workers and governments would attempt, beginning in the 1880s, through the residential school system.

The residential school system was based on the notion that assimilation was best for First Nations people and that the best method of assimilation was to remove children from their homes and teach them the ways of Euro-Canadian society in schools where they also lived. The Canadian government made the rules, such as mandatory attendance, and

Church and totem pole, Old Masset. The pole, carved by Robert Davidson and raised in 1969, was the first to be erected in the village in nearly a hundred years. Churches continue to be central to many First Nations communities.

provided most of the funding, while the Roman Catholic, Anglican, Methodist, Baptist, Presbyterian, and United churches operated the schools. The policy of most residential schools was first to break the children of all cultural ties, such as language, family, and traditional lifeways, and then to re-educate them in Christian and Euro-Canadian ways. It was common for children to be given new names, to be physically abused for speaking their native language, and to be taught that the ways of their parents were evil.

The residential school system had a severe impact on First Nations people and their cultures. Reports of physical, sexual, and emotional abuse of First Nations children attending residential schools began in the late nineteenth century and have continued throughout the twentieth century. The schools also contributed to the loss of many traditional lifeways, including languages and knowledge about healing, parenting, and social relations. Extended periods of school residence frequently led to family breakdown. Children returning from school were often unable to communicate with their parents and had little in common with them.

First Nations children attending residential schools usually received a poorer education than other children. Even in the mid-twentieth century government spending on First Nations children in residential schools was less than 25 percent of that for non-First Nations children. Also, children in most residential schools received less education in academic subjects than did non-First Nations children. Instead many residential schools focused on instruction in farming and trades.

The impact of residential schools has long been a source of controversy. It is clear that many First Nations people did not want to be part of the system. It is also evident, however, that some First Nations people saw attendance at the schools as a useful means of learning how to co-exist with Euro-Canadians. As well, some First Nations converts to Christianity saw the residential schools as an effective way of spreading the faith.

As a mechanism for assimilating First Nations people into Euro-Canadian society, the residential school system is widely acknowledged to have failed and some of the churches that operated the schools have publicly apologized. As long ago as 1947 Diamond Jenness, a prominent anthropologist, declared that the residential schools were a failure and recommended their abolition, but the last residential school in British Columbia did not close until 1984.

Government Relations with First Nations

One of the most important documents governing relations between First Nations and the governments of British Columbia and Canada is the **Royal Proclamation** issued by King George III of England in 1763 (Appendix 3). The proclamation was issued to maintain peace and a sense of order between British subjects and First Nations in North America. It asserted that the First Nations of North America had existing rights and established the system of surrendering those rights by treaty. While some people view relations with the First Nations of British Columbia as outside the intent of the Royal Proclamation because no European had yet been to the area now known as British Columbia when the proclamation was written, others see it as a guarantee of the rights of all First Nations on the continent.

Before the mid-nineteenth century there was relatively little conflict over aboriginal rights in what is now British Columbia, probably because the colonial government vested responsibility for relations with First Nations with traders. The traders were focused on maintaining exchange networks and had little interest in broader issues of aboriginal rights, including the ramifications of the Royal Proclamation and treaties.

Colonial government policies, including the Royal Proclamation, began to have a significant impact on First Nations in the mid-nineteenth century with the official establishment of British colonies in what is now British Columbia. Vancouver Island was made a British colony in 1849, and all of what is now British Columbia was made a colony in 1858.

One of the most influential people of the late nineteenth century in relations between First Nations and colonial governments was James Douglas. Douglas was a long-time Hudson's Bay Company employee with an extensive history of work in the region. While with the Hudson's Bay Company, Douglas had worked with First Nations on Vancouver Island and what was to become the mainland of British Columbia. Later, as governor of Vancouver Island from 1851 to 1858 and all of what is now British Columbia from 1858 until his retirement in 1864, he was responsible for government relations with First Nations. Following the spirit of the Royal Proclamation, Douglas made fourteen treaties with nations on Vancouver Island between 1851 and 1854, known as the **Douglas treaties.** The treaties allowed the nations continuing rights to hunt and fish in their traditional territories. Neither the British government nor the provincial assembly would provide the necessary funds for further treaties after 1854 but Douglas did continue to confer with natives and to lay out reserves.

Douglas is usually portrayed as sympathetic to First Nations concerns. He recognized aboriginal rights, consulted First Nations about the laying out of reserves, and sought peacekeepers with knowledge of First Nations to maintain order and resolve conflicts between native people and gold seekers and settlers throughout the province. Douglas also advised First Nations to seek retribution or compensation for perceived wrongs through British law.

Following Douglas's retirement in 1864, the person responsible for government relations with First Nations was Joseph

Trutch. As chief commissioner for lands and works and later as lieutenant governor, Trutch was active in creating policy until his retirement in 1880. He viewed First Nations as a hindrance to the development of the province. He often spoke of First Nations people in a derogatory manner, reduced the size of their reserves, and denied all forms of aboriginal rights. In no sense whatsoever did Trutch follow the spirit of the Royal Proclamation.

The allocation of reserves, which began in the mid-nineteenth century, involves both provincial and federal governments. Throughout the early 1860s Governor James Douglas established the reserve system in British Columbia. His policy is unclear but indications are that he viewed ten acres per family as a minimum allocation. When Trutch assumed responsibility for First Nations he arbitrarily decreased the size of some reserves established by Douglas and set ten acres per family as a maximum for new reserves. In comparison, the standard formulas used for Ontario and the prairie provinces were eighty and 640 acres per family respectively. Although there is some doubt whether the federal government knew of BC government policies and practices regarding First Nations, including the ten-acre maximum, the terms of union entrenched the formula. In 1924 the federal government passed a bill that made decreasing the size of reserves without the consent of First Nations legal.

When British Columbia joined Canada in 1871, the primary responsibility for government relations with First Nations was transferred to the federal government. Of the many federal government acts, policies, accords, and commissions affecting the First Nations of British Columbia, several stand out: the Indian Act, the Statement of the Government of Canada on Indian Policy, the Canadian Constitution, the Meech Lake Accord, the Charlottetown Accord, and the Royal Commission on Aboriginal Peoples.

First appearing in 1876, and having undergone several revisions since, the Indian Act governs relations between First Nations and the Canadian government. Many people view the act as paternalistic and detrimental to First Nations people in Canada. Governing such things as the acquisition of status, election of councils, use of reserves, management of money, and education, the Indian Act is viewed by some as structuring inequality and poverty. It is also often seen as a mechanism to destroy First Nations' cultures and to restrict protests and litigation. Past versions of the Indian Act made potlatches and the pursuit of land claims illegal.

Prohibitions against the potlatch were first introduced in the 1880s and were subsequently made stronger in later revisions. Section 140 of the 1927 version of the Indian Act states:

> Every Indian or other person who engages in, or assists in celebrating or encourages either directly or indirectly another to celebrate any Indian festival, dance or other ceremony of which the giving away or paying or giving back of money, goods or articles of any sort forms a part, or is a feature, whether such gift of money, goods or articles takes place before, at, or after the celebration of the same ... is guilty of an offence and is liable on summary conviction to imprisonment for a term not exceeding six months and not less than two months.

Many people went to prison for participating in potlatches and many of the masks and other objects present at potlatches were confiscated. Some confiscated items were sent to museums while others were either kept or sold by government workers. Potlatching remained illegal until 1951.

In response to increasing protests from First Nations in the early nineteenth century over their rights, the federal government legislated against hiring lawyers to pursue land claims. Section 141 of the 1927 version of the Indian Act states:

> Every person who, without the consent of the Superin-
> tendent General expressed in writing, receives, obtains,
> solicits, or requests from any Indian any payment or
> contribution or promise of any payment or contribu-
> tion for the purpose of raising a fund or providing
> money for the prosecution of any claim which the tribe
> or band of Indians to which such Indian belongs, or of
> which he is a member, has or is represented to have for
> the recovery of any claim or money for the benefit of
> the said tribe or band, shall be guilty of an offence and
> liable upon summary conviction for each such offence
> to a penalty not exceeding two hundred dollars and not
> less than fifty dollars or to imprisonment for any term
> not exceeding two months.

Notwithstanding the potentially detrimental effects of the Indian Act on First Nations people, many also see positive consequences. It gives special status to First Nations people, it offers some protection of aboriginal rights, such as the maintenance of reserves, and it provides such benefits as medical care and education.

In 1969 Jean Chrétien, then minister of Indian affairs in the federal government, released a document entitled State-ment of the Government of Canada on Indian Policy, more widely known as the White Paper. It proposed the complete assimilation of First Nations people into Canadian culture by the abolition of Indian status, the Indian Act, and the Department of Indian Affairs. Reaction to the White Paper by First Nations in British Columbia and elsewhere in Canada was negative and it was subsequently withdrawn. While they had not been pleased with the paternalistic nature of federal government policies concerning their affairs, First Nations leaders viewed the proposals as an elimination of their legislative protection and a denial of aboriginal rights. Leaders were also angry that they had not been consulted by the federal government about proposed changes in policy, as had been promised. Because the White Paper proposed assimilation, in which there would be no special status or rights, it is somewhat ironic that it provided a focus of opposition that bonded many First Nations. The creation of the Union of British Columbia Indian Chiefs, for example, a group still politically active in aboriginal rights issues today, was one response to the White Paper.

Another important federal government act in relation to First Nations was the patriation and revision of the Canadian Constitution in 1982. Section 35 of the Constitution states:

(1) The existing aboriginal and treaty rights of the aboriginal peoples of Canada are hereby recognized and affirmed.

(2) In this Act, 'aboriginal peoples of Canada' includes the **Indian, Inuit** and **Métis** peoples of Canada.

(3) For greater certainty, in subsection (1) 'treaty rights' includes rights that now exist by way of land claims agreement or may be so acquired.

(4) Notwithstanding any other provision of this Act, the aboriginal and treaty rights referred to in subsection (1) are guaranteed equally to male and female persons.

Subsections (1) and (2) were part of the original Constitution of 1982. Subsections (3) and (4) were added by the Constitution Amendment Proclamation, 1983. Recognition of aboriginal rights in the Constitution has prompted various court cases and treaty negotiations. Although it affirms the existence of aboriginal rights, definition of those rights has been left to the courts.

Another part of the Constitution with significant implications for First Nations is the Canadian Charter of Rights and Freedoms. Section 25 of the Charter states:

> The guarantee in this Charter of certain rights and freedoms shall not be construed so as to abrogate or derogate from any aboriginal, treaty or other rights or freedoms that pertain to the aboriginal peoples of Canada including
> (a) any rights or freedoms that have been recognized by the Royal Proclamation of October 7, 1763; and
> (b) any rights or freedoms that now exist by way of land claims settlement.

The Charter also guarantees equality between the sexes, which led the federal government in 1985 to pass Bill C-31, An Act to Amend the Indian Act, eliminating sexual discrimination in the act. Prior to that a woman and her children faced automatic loss of Indian status if she married a non-Indian man. Bill C-31 is also significant because it provided First Nations with the option of controlling their own membership – determining who could be a member of the First Nation – and allowed for the restoration of status to those who had either voluntarily relinquished it or had lost it through previous legislation.

Although the Meech Lake Accord was blocked and the Charlottetown Accord was defeated in a national referendum, both had important implications for First Nations in British Columbia and elsewhere in Canada. Discussions among politicians, aboriginal leaders, and the public raised the profile of First Nations people, organizations, and issues.

Formulated in 1987 between the prime minister and provincial premiers, the Meech Lake Accord described Quebec as a 'distinct society' but failed to recognize the concerns of aboriginal people in Canada. Aboriginal leaders articulated their concerns to the Canadian public and helped block passage of the accord in 1990, to the pleasure of many First Nations people and other Canadians opposed to the accord for a variety of reasons.

At least partly due to the issues raised about the Meech Lake Accord, the federal government invited aboriginal leaders to participate in the development of the Charlottetown Accord. As a result, First Nations issues, including recognition of an inherent right of self-government, were addressed in the document. Although the Charlottetown Accord was defeated in a 1992 referendum, the role of aboriginal people in the process was significant. It was the first time that they had been treated as equals in such important discussions about the relations between First Nations and governments and the future of the country.

In 1991 the federal government established a royal commission, made up of both aboriginal and non-aboriginal people, to investigate issues concerning aboriginal peoples. After five years of study and at an estimated cost of $58 million – the most expensive royal commission in Canadian history – the commission released its five-volume report in late 1996. Its central conclusion was that 'the main policy direction, pursued for more than 150 years, first by colonial then by Canadian governments, has been wrong.' Major recommendations included the creation of an aboriginal parliament and increased spending on First Nations programs for the next fifteen to twenty years, presumably improving economic and social conditions to the extent that the short-term influx of money will lead to long-term financial savings for all Canadians.

In January 1998 the federal government made its first official response to the report of the royal commission, stating, 'The government of Canada today formally expresses to all Aboriginal people in Canada our profound regret for past actions of the federal government which have contributed to these difficult pages in the history of our relationships together.' As well as the apology, the government created a $350-million healing fund and promised an additional $250 million, spread out over four years, over current funding for aboriginal peoples. The commission report recommended an increase in spending of $1.5 to $2 billion per year over the next fifteen to twenty years.

Assertions of Aboriginal Rights

First Nations in British Columbia have a long history of asserting their rights by protests, petitions, confrontations, litigation, and negotiation. Throughout the late nineteenth and early twentieth centuries, First Nations across the province held large assemblies protesting the denial of aboriginal rights, lack of government willingness to negotiate treaties, and the small size of their reserves. The assemblies sometimes led to formal petitions to provincial, federal, and British governments, and representatives of First Nations travelled to Victoria, Ottawa, and England to seek redress (Appendix 4). The routine response of governments was inaction.

Confrontation has long been used to assert aboriginal rights in the province. There are many stories of First Nations people resisting the actions of Euro-Canadians by making threats, confiscating surveying equipment, and resorting to violence. One of the best known examples is the 'Chilcotin wars,' in which more than a dozen road builders and settlers were killed by members of the Tsilhqot'in nation attempting to protect their land and lifeways in 1864. Confrontation in the form of blockades became common in the 1980s and 1990s. Blockades were erected in British Columbia in 1990 to show support for those involved in the Oka crisis in Quebec. Most often, however, blocking roads and rail lines in the province has been a means of pressuring governments and private companies to negotiate outstanding issues and claims, often with some success and rarely escalating into violence.

The most violent confrontation in recent years occurred in 1995 at Gustafsen Lake, near 100 Mile House in the Cariboo. The right to occupy a sacred site was at the heart of a conflict between a few dozen First Nations people and their supporters and approximately 400 RCMP officers and military personnel. Although there were injuries, the standoff ended without anyone being killed. Charges against fourteen First Nations people and four of their non-native supporters ranged from attempted murder to criminal mischief and possession of weapons. A 1997 jury verdict resulted in four people being convicted of possessing weapons and of mischief endangering life, eleven people being convicted of wilful mischief, and three people being acquitted.

Many First Nations have chosen to assert their ideas of aboriginal rights through the courts. Significant cases include *Calder* (1973), *Sparrow* (1990), and *Delgamuukw* (1997).

In the *Calder* case, the Nisga'a Tribal Council asserted that the title to their lands had never been **extinguished.** The case is significant because it was the first Supreme Court of Canada decision concerning aboriginal rights in Canada, it used the Royal Proclamation in support of the claim, and it influenced the federal government's policy on negotiation. The decision affirmed that aboriginal rights did exist at the time of European settlement. Although the six judges of the Supreme Court who heard the case were unanimous that there were existing rights at the time of initial contact with Europeans, they were split evenly on whether those rights had subsequently been extinguished. The decision affirming the existence of aboriginal rights was significant enough that the federal government immediately changed its policy on dealing with aboriginal rights from one of non-negotiation to one of negotiation. Thus, after close to 100 years since the Nisga'a initiated their claim, in the mid-1970s the federal government finally agreed to enter into negotiations. An **agreement-in-principle** was created in 1996 (Appendix 5).

The *Sparrow* case is significant because it used the Constitution as an affirmation of aboriginal rights. Ronald Sparrow, an elder of the Musqueam Nation in Vancouver, was charged and subsequently convicted of illegal fishing. The Supreme Court of Canada overturned the conviction, ruling that the Constitution protected aboriginal rights to fisheries. The court further ruled that any government regulations that infringe on those rights must be constitutionally justified, that aboriginal rights are capable of evolving, that aboriginal rights should be interpreted in a generous and liberal manner, and that the right of aboriginal peoples to fish for food should be given priority over commercial and sport fishing.

The *Delgamuukw* case began in 1984 when thirty-five Gitxsan and thirteen Wet'suwet'en hereditary chiefs claimed ownership of their traditional territories, the right to self-government, and compensation for loss of lands and resources. In 1991, after three years of testimony, Chief Justice Allan McEachern of the Supreme Court of British Columbia ruled that aboriginal rights had been extinguished during colonial times. The hereditary chiefs took the decision to the BC Court of Appeal, which ruled that the Gitxsan and Wet'suwet'en people did have aboriginal rights but that those rights were non-exclusive. It recommended that the scope of the rights would best be determined through negotiation rather than through litigation. The Gitxsan and Wet'suwet'en subsequently took the case to the Supreme Court of Canada, which in December 1997 ordered a new trial and ruled on several issues arising in the case, including the nature of **aboriginal title** and the rules for proving its existence. The Supreme Court also asserted that the lower courts should give more weight to the oral histories of First Nations peoples and that governments may only infringe on aboriginal title if they have a 'compelling and substantial legislative objective.' Further, when governments do infringe thus, First Nations must receive 'fair compensation.'

Negotiations in the 1990s

Most First Nations in British Columbia never signed treaties. Notable exceptions are the fourteen treaties made by Governor Douglas in the early 1850s and Treaty 8, made by the federal government in 1899. Treaty 8 dealt mostly with groups living in Alberta and the Northwest Territories but also included nations of Saskatchewan and northeastern British Columbia.

Despite federal involvement in resolving claims of the Nisga'a, the provincial government refused until 1990 to participate in negotiations with First Nations. From Joseph Trutch onward, spokespeople for the provincial government either denied the existence of aboriginal rights or declared that if aboriginal rights did exist they were a federal responsibility. In 1990, however, the provincial government agreed to participate in a treaty-making process. Representatives of First Nations and the provincial and federal governments recommended establishing the British Columbia Claims Task Force to determine how negotiations should proceed. Key recommendations of the task force, implemented in 1992, were the creation of a six-stage process for negotiations and a treaty commission to oversee it.

The six-stage treaty negotiation process is as follows: a statement of intent by the First Nation to negotiate a treaty; preparation for negotiations; negotiation of a framework agreement; negotiation of an agreement-in-principle; negotiation to finalize a treaty; and implementation of the treaty. The Treaty Commission consists of five commissioners: two chosen by the First Nations Summit, consisting of nations that have agreed to participate in the process; one chosen by the federal government; one chosen by the provincial government; and a chief commissioner chosen jointly by all three parties. The Treaty Commission coordinates the start of negotiations, assesses whether all three parties are ready to begin, monitors their progress, allocates funds to First

Nations to assist their preparations, and keeps a public record of the status of negotiations. The funds are 80 percent loans and 20 percent contributions. The Treaty Commission also assesses whether the parties involved have a mandate to negotiate treaties and whether mechanisms have been established to consult non-aboriginal interests. The mechanisms include regular meetings between government negotiators, the province-wide Treaty Negotiation Advisory Committee (TNAC), and regional or local Regional Advisory Committees (RACs), which represent public, private, and business interests of non-aboriginal British Columbians.

Because the Nisga'a negotiations were under way before the Treaty Commission was established they are not governed by it but nevertheless follow the same basic plan. Approximately 70 percent of the BC registered Indian population is represented in treaty negotiations. Some nations are negotiating individually whereas others are working through tribal councils or other affiliations (Appendix 6).

Reconstructed pithouse at Secwepemc Archaeological Heritage Park. Four full-size pithouses have been reconstructed adjacent to the prehistoric village.

Economic and Cultural Initiatives

First Nations economic initiatives have proliferated in British Columbia in recent years. In the tourism industry alone, for example, there are more than 200 First Nations-owned and -operated businesses. Other industries in which First Nations have become competitive include, but are by no means limited to, fishing, forestry, and land development. Some ventures are wholly owned and operated by one or more First Nations; others are operated in partnership with governments or private-sector companies.

Many First Nations have implemented programs in language, education, media, and health. Numerous programs have been designed to revitalize languages, and schools with First Nations teachers are now common on reserves. Various postsecondary First Nations institutes and programs

Aboriginal students from the Sk'lep School on the Kamloops Reserve visiting the 1997 SCES/ SFU Archaeology Field School Excavations nearby. Many First Nations operate their own schools on reserve, where in addition to the regular BC curriculum students are given opportunities to learn about First Nations languages and cultures.

have also been established, such as the Institute of Indigenous Government and the Nicola Valley Institute of Technology. Several First Nations have published books about their cultures and more than a dozen newspapers, such as *Kahtou* and the *Secwepemc News*, serve First Nations communities at both the provincial and the local level. Many First Nations have founded healing centres and cultural education centres. Examples are the Coqualeetza Cultural Education Centre, the K'San Village and Museum, and Secwepemc Native Heritage Park.

Many First Nations have also been involved in initiatives to repatriate cultural and human remains. Tens of thousands of artifacts and hundreds of human skeletons have been removed from archaeological sites and taken from First Nations territories by anthropologists, collectors, and government agents. Many of these were taken unlawfully and have been stored in museums and private collections around the world. Some First Nations have been successful in getting skeletal remains returned for reburial and have built museums to house artifacts given back by museums. The U'Mista Cultural Centre at Alert Bay, for example, was built primarily to house repatriated Kwakwaka'wakw items confiscated in the early twentieth century and stored in the Canadian Museum of Civilization.

Outstanding Issues

Few people familiar with the last 200 years of BC history would argue that First Nations people in the province have been treated fairly. Unfair dealings were certainly not unique to British Columbia, however, and in many ways were typical of the treatment aboriginal peoples received from members of colonizing nations throughout the world. As are non-native people everywhere, those in British Columbia today are coming to terms with past social and legal injustices inflicted upon First Nations. Some ways of dealing with those issues have included public education and apologies, government inquiries and commissions, the return of human remains and artifacts, and the current treaty negotiation process.

Another way of dealing with compensating past legal injustices is a process known as **specific claims.** Unlike broad claims of aboriginal rights (sometimes known as **comprehensive claims**), specific claims include accusations against governments and their agents or corporations for such things as the mismanagement of leases and reserves. These claims are often referred to as a breach of trusteeship or **fiduciary duty.** Most claims relate to activities that occurred in the late nineteenth and early twentieth centuries but were not brought forward until recently. The settlements are usually for less than a million dollars but a few have been quite large. In December 1997, for example, the Osoyoos First Nation approved a settlement of $11.7 million as compensation for the illegal sale of reserve land. The current value of the land is about $60 million. In early 1998 there were about 150 outstanding specific claims by First Nations in British Columbia.

The full impact of the Royal Commission on Aboriginal Peoples and the Supreme Court of Canada *Delgamuukw* decision remains unknown. Both initially appear to favour First Nations but the full ramifications will probably take years to emerge. Although the government's initial response to the report of the Royal Commission was an apology and a commitment of several hundred million dollars, the budgeting details remain vague and the response fails to address many substantive issues and the more than 400 recommendations in the report. The *Delgamuukw* decision will undoubtedly influence assertions of aboriginal rights both in the way that court cases are undertaken and perhaps also in treaty negotiations. Numerous issues are attached to current treaty negotiations. Many First Nations have yet to resolve overlapping claims, and many non-native British Columbians are worried about the economic, social, and political implications of treaties.

One issue likely to become increasingly newsworthy in coming years is settlement with First Nations not participating in treaty negotiation. Approximately 30 percent of 'registered' First Nations people in British Columbia are not represented in the treaty-making process. Leadership of some First Nations has expressed no interest in participating in the negotiations using the existing framework – the six-stage process involving representatives of both the federal and provincial governments – but remains determined to assert aboriginal rights.

Another issue liable to become prominent is the treatment of 'non-status' First Nations people. Although they have suffered past injustices equal to or greater than the ones inflicted on those with status, First Nations people without status are at a greater disadvantage. They will not benefit from treaty negotiations and have no similar avenue to address the same issues.

First Nations are continually changing. Some past lifeways have been deliberately discarded or lost and new technologies and ideas from non-native cultures are frequently added. Economic, social, political, and ideological aspects of First Nations often comprise a mixture of traditional and modern elements, reflecting strong links between the past and

Nuxalk woman wearing a mask by Ray Martin,
1997. Although often marketed to non-native
people, carved masks and other forms of art
remain important elements of First Nations
cultures today. Illustrated here is the link between
past and present.

present, traditional and modern. While fishers and hunters
often use modern technology, for example, where they fish
and hunt often depends on rights that have passed through
many generations. Leadership is often based on both the
modern model of elected chiefs and councillors and the more
traditional model of hereditary leadership and consultation
with elders. It is not unusual for people to incorporate elements of traditional values and beliefs with aspects of modern Christianity.

First Nations issues will probably remain prominent in British Columbia media well into the twenty-first century. Many First Nations will seek compensation and determination of their aboriginal rights through the courts, and new agreements between First Nations and the provincial and federal governments will be negotiated. Because some non-natives perceive First Nations gains in monetary compensation and increased control over land and resources as coming at their own expense, conflicts between non-natives and First Nations will continue. Similarly, because no single organization represents the interest of all First Nations people in British Columbia, and because leaders often disagree, conflicts between First Nations will continue. As they enter education, media, anthropology, and other academic fields in increasing numbers, First Nations people will be heard on many non-political issues, such as culture, art, and health. For those with an interest in the First Nations people and cultures of British Columbia, interesting times are ahead.

Suggested Reading

Articles on First Nations history and contemporary issues regularly appear in *B.C. Studies*. Robin Fisher's *Contact and Conflict: Indian-European Relations in British Columbia, 1774-1890*, 2nd ed. (Vancouver: UBC Press 1992) and Paul Tennant's *Aboriginal Peoples and Politics: The Indian Land Question in British Columbia, 1849-1989* (Vancouver: UBC Press 1990) are both highly recommended. Christopher McKee provides an informed view of treaty negotiations in *Treaty Talks in British Columbia: Negotiating a Mutually Beneficial Future* (Vancouver: UBC Press 1996). Dara Culhane's *The Pleasure of the Crown: Anthropology, Law and First Nations* (Vancouver: Talon Books 1998) includes lengthy commentary on the *Delgamuukw* case.

Appendices

The First Nations of British Columbia

The First Nations described here qualify as bands under the Indian Act. The following are also considered to be ethnic groups unto themselves: Comox, Haisla, Heiltsuk, Homalco, Klahoose, Nat'oot'en, Nuxalk, Oweekeno, Sechelt, Sliammon, Squamish, Tahltan, and Tsleil Waututh. Given here for each nation are the number of reserves it holds, their location, the origin of its name where available, the total registered population, and the larger ethnic group to which the nation belongs, if known. The descriptions are based primarily on information provided by the provincial Ministry of Aboriginal Affairs and Indian and Northern Affairs Canada.

Adams Lake
Eight reserves in south-central British Columbia, near Chase. Named after a chief who was given the name Adam. Total registered population approximately 600. Secwepemc ethnic group.

Ahousaht
Twenty-five reserves, with most members living on Flores Island, off the west coast of Vancouver Island. Possible meanings of the name include 'facing opposite from the ocean' or 'people living with their backs to the land and mountains.' Total registered population approximately 1,400. Nuu'chah'nulth ethnic group.

Aitchelitz
Three reserves in the Fraser Valley, near Chilliwack. Named with the Halkomelem word for 'bottom,' associated with a creek that goes around the bottom of Chilliwack Mountain. Total registered population less than 100. Halq'emeylem ethnic group.

Alexandria
> Fourteen reserves in central British Columbia, near Alexandria. Total registered population approximately 200. Dakelh ethnic group.

Alexis Creek
> Thirty-seven reserves in central British Columbia, near Alexis Creek. Total registered population approximately 500. Tsilhqot'in ethnic group.

Alkali Lake. See *Esketemc*

Anaham (Tl'etinqox)
> Nineteen reserves in central British Columbia, west of Williams Lake. Total registered population approximately 1,100. Tsilhqot'in ethnic group.

Anderson Lake
> Six reserves near Lillooet. Total registered population approximately 300. Stl'atl'imx ethnic group.

Ashcroft
> Four reserves near Ashcroft, in south-central British Columbia. Total registered population approximately 200. Nlaka'pamux ethnic group.

Beecher Bay
> Eight reserves on southern Vancouver Island. Total registered population approximately 200. Straits Salish ethnic group.

Bella Bella. See *Heiltsuk*

Bella Coola. See *Nuxalk*

Blueberry River
> Two reserves in northeastern British Columbia. The Fort St John Band (formerly known as St John Beaver Band) split in two in 1977, forming the Doig River and Blueberry River bands. Total registered population approximately 300. Dunne-za ethnic group.

Bonaparte
> Nine reserves in south-central British Columbia, near Cache

Creek. Total registered population approximately 700. Secwepemc ethnic group.

Boothroyd (Chomok)
Nineteen reserves in the Fraser Canyon area. Formerly known as the Chomok Band. Total registered population approximately 300. Nlaka'pamux ethnic group.

Boston Bar
Twelve reserves in the Fraser Canyon area. Total registered population approximately 200. Nlaka'pamux ethnic group.

Bridge River
Four reserves near Lillooet. Total registered population approximately 300. Stl'atl'imx ethnic group.

Broman Lake (Omineca)
Eleven reserves in central British Columbia. In 1984 the Omineca split into two bands, the Nee-Tahi-Buhn and Broman Lake. Total registered population approximately 200. Wet'suwet'en ethnic group.

Burns Lake
Four reserves in central British Columbia, near Burns Lake. Total registered population approximately 100. Dakelh ethnic group.

Burrard. See *Tsleil Waututh*

Campbell River. See *We Wai kum, Kwiakah*

Canim Lake
Six reserves in south-central British Columbia, near Canim Lake. Total registered population approximately 500. Secwepemc ethnic group.

Canoe Creek
Twelve reserves in south-central British Columbia, near Canoe Creek. Amalgamated with former Dog Creek Band. Total registered population approximately 600. Secwepemc ethnic group.

Canyon City. See *Gitwinksihlkw*

Cape Mudge. See *We Wai Kai*

Cayoose Creek

Three reserves in south-central British Columbia, near Lillooet. Total registered population approximately 200. Stl'atl'imx ethnic group.

Chawathil (Hope)

Five reserves in south-central British Columbia, near Hope. Formerly known as the Hope Band. Total registered population approximately 300. Halq'emeylem ethnic group.

Cheam

Two reserves near Chilliwack in the Fraser Valley. The name may be translated as 'the place to get strawberries.' Total registered population approximately 300. Halq'emeylem ethnic group.

Chehalis

Four reserves near the Harrison River in the Upper Fraser Valley. Possible translations are 'the place one reaches after ascending the rapids' and 'where the chest of the canoe grounds on a sandbar.' Total registered population approximately 800. Halq'emeylem ethnic group.

Chemainus

Four reserves on Vancouver Island. The name may be translated as 'bitten breast,' probably in reference to the geography of the area, which to some people resembles a man with a cleft in his chest. Total registered population approximately 800. Hul'qumi'num ethnic group.

Cheslatta

Seventeen reserves in central British Columbia. Total registered population approximately 200. Dakelh ethnic group.

Chomok. See *Boothroyd*

Clayoquot. See *Tla-o-qui-aht*

Clinton. See *Whispering Pines*

Coldwater

Three reserves in the Nicola Valley, near Merritt. Total

registered population approximately 600. Nlaka'pamux
ethnic group.

Columbia Lake

Two reserves in southeastern British Columbia. Total registered population approximately 200. Ktunaxa ethnic group.

Comox

Four reserves on eastern Vancouver Island, near Comox.
Name translates as 'place of abundance.' Total registered
population approximately 300.

Cook's Ferry

Twenty-five reserves in the south-central interior of British
Columbia, near Spences Bridge. Total registered population approximately 300. Nlaka'pamux ethnic group.

Coquitlam. See *Kwayhquitlim*

Cowichan

Nine reserves near Duncan on Vancouver Island. Cowichan
may be translated as 'warm country.' Total registered population approximately 2,800. Hul'qumi'num ethnic group.

Cowichan Lake

One reserve on Lake Cowichan. Total registered population less than 100. Hul'qumi'num ethnic group.

Deadman's Creek. See *Skeetchestn*

Dease River

Although the nation has a settlement in northeastern British Columbia, near Good Hope Lake, it is administered by
the Yukon regional office of Indian and Northern Affairs
Canada. Total registered population approximately 200.
Kaska ethnic group.

Ditidaht (Nitinaht)

Fourteen reserves on central Vancouver Island. Changed
name from Nitinaht in 1984. Total registered population
approximately 500. Sometimes considered to be within
the Nuu'chah'nulth ethnic group.

Doig River

Two reserves near Fort St John in northeastern British

Columbia. The Fort St John Band split in two in 1977 to form the Blueberry River and Doig River bands. Total registered population approximately 200. Dunne-za and Sekani ethnic groups.

Douglas

Three reserves at the head of Harrison Lake. The name derives from Governor Douglas. Total registered population approximately 200. Stl'atl'imx ethnic group.

Ehattesaht

Nine reserves on northern Vancouver Island, near Campbell River. Total registered population approximately 200. Nuu'chah'nulth ethnic group.

Esketemc (Alkali Lake)

Nineteen reserves in central British Columbia, south of Williams Lake. Formerly known as the Alkali Lake Band. Total registered population approximately 600. Secwepemc ethnic group.

Esquimalt

One reserve on southern Vancouver Island, near Victoria. Esquimalt derives from a word meaning 'place of gradually shoaling water.' Total registered population approximately 200. Straits Salish ethnic group.

Fort George. See *Lheidli T'enneh*

Fort Nelson

Four reserves in northeastern British Columbia, near Fort Nelson. Originally known as the Slave Indian Band. Some of the membership left in 1974 to form the Prophet River Band. Total registered population approximately 600. Dene-thah and Sekani ethnic groups.

Fort Rupert. See *Kwakiutl*

Fort Ware

Three reserves in northeastern British Columbia, near Fort Ware. Formerly part of the Finlay River Band (which itself resulted from the amalgamation of the first Fort Ware Band and the Fort Graham Band), which split to form the Ingenika and Fort Ware bands. Total registered population approximately 500. Sekani ethnic group.

Fountain. See *Xaxli'p*

Fraser Lake. See *Nadleh Whut'en*

Gitanmaax

Five reserves in northwestern British Columbia, near Hazelton. The name means 'people who fish with burning torches.' Total registered population approximately 1,600. Gitxsan ethnic group.

Gitanyow

Three reserves in northwestern British Columbia, near Kitwanga. Total registered population approximately 600. Gitxsan ethnic group.

Git'k'a'ata (Hartley Bay)

Fifteen reserves near the mainland coast, south of Prince Rupert. Total registered population approximately 600. Tsimshian ethnic group.

Gitlakdamix

Thirty-two reserves in northwestern British Columbia, near the Nass River. Total registered population approximately 1,500. Nisga'a ethnic group.

Gitsegukla

Four reserves near the Skeena River in northwestern British Columbia. Total registered population approximately 700. Gitxsan ethnic group.

Gitwangak

Seven reserves in northwestern British Columbia. Gitwangak may be translated as 'place of rabbits.' Total registered population approximately 900. Gitxsan ethnic group.

Gitwinksihlkw (Canyon City)

Six reserves near the Nass River in northwestern British Columbia. Formerly known as the Canyon City Band. Total registered population approximately 400. Nisga'a ethnic group.

Glen Vowell. See Sikokoak

Greenville. See Lakalzap

Gwa'sala-Nakwaxda'xw (Tsulquate)

Twenty-six reserves on the central mainland coast. Formerly known as Tsulquate and part of the Kwawkewlth Band (now the Kwakiutl Nation), which subdivided in 1981. Total registered population approximately 500. Kwakwaka'wakw ethnic group.

Hagwilget

Two reserves in northwestern British Columbia, near New Hazelton. Translated as 'gentle or quiet people.' Total registered population approximately 600. Wet'suwet'en ethnic group.

Haisla. See Kitamaat

Halalt

Two reserves on southern Vancouver Island, near Duncan. Total registered population approximately 200. Hul'qumi'num ethnic group.

Halfway River

One reserve in northeastern British Columbia. Formed in 1977 from the split of the Hudson Hope band into the West Moberly and Halfway River bands. Total registered population approximately 200. Dunne-za ethnic group.

Hartley Bay. See Git'k'a'ata

Heiltsuk (Bella Bella)

Twenty-two reserves on the central mainland coast. Formerly known as the Bella Bella. Heiltsuk translates as 'to speak or act correctly.' Total registered population approximately 1,900.

Hesquiaht

Six reserves on the central west coast of Vancouver Island. Total registered population approximately 600. Nuu'chah'nulth ethnic group.

High Bar

Three reserves near the Fraser River in south-central

British Columbia. Total registered population approximately 100. Secwepemc ethnic group.

Homalco

Eleven reserves on the central mainland coast and Vancouver Island. Total registered population approximately 400.

Hope. See *Chawathil*

Huu-ay-aht (Ohiaht)

Thirteen reserves on southwestern Vancouver Island. Total registered population approximately 500. Nuu'chah'nulth ethnic group.

Ingenika. See *Tsay Keh Dene*

Iskut

Three reserves in northwestern British Columbia, near Telegraph Creek. Total registered population approximately 500. Tahltan ethnic group.

Kamloops

Six reserves near Kamloops in southern British Columbia. The name translates as 'meeting of the waters.' Total registered population approximately 800. Secwepemc ethnic group.

Kanaka Bar

Six reserves near the Fraser Canyon area. Total registered population approximately 200. Nlaka'pamux ethnic group.

Katzie

Five reserves in the lower Fraser Valley. Total registered population approximately 400. Halq'emeylem ethnic group.

Ka:'yu:'K't'h'/Che:K'tles7et'h' (Kyuquot)

Twenty-seven reserves near the northwest coast of Vancouver Island. The Kyuquot and Checleset bands amalgamated in 1962, retaining the Kyuquot name. Total registered population approximately 400. Nuu'chah'nulth ethnic group.

Kincolith

Thirty-four reserves on the north mainland coast. Total

registered population approximately 1,600. Nisga'a ethnic group.

Kingcome Inlet. See *Tsawataineuk*

Kispiox

Ten reserves in northwestern British Columbia. Kispiox is derived from the Nisga'a name for a Gitx̱san village, meaning 'people of the hiding place.' Population approximately 1,200. Gitx̱san ethnic group.

Kitamaat (Haisla)

Eighteen reserves near Kitimat. Kitamaat derives from a Tsimshian word meaning 'people of the falling snow.' Total registered population approximately 1,400.

Kitasoo (Klemtu)

Fifteen reserves on the north-central mainland coast. Total registered population approximately 500. Tsimshian ethnic group.

Kitkatla

Twenty-one reserves on the north mainland coast, near Prince Rupert. Total registered population approximately 1,300. Tsimshian ethnic group.

Kitselas

Nine reserves near Terrace. Total registered population approximately 400. Tsimshian ethnic group.

Kitsumkalum

Four reserves near Terrace. The name may be translated as 'people of the plateau.' Total registered population approximately 600. Tsimshian ethnic group.

Klahoose

Ten reserves in the Johnston Strait area of the mainland coast. Total registered population approximately 300. Sometimes considered part of the Kwakwaka'wakw ethnic group.

Klemtu. See *Kitasoo*

Kluskus

Seventeen reserves in central British Columbia, near Quesnel.

The name translates as 'place of small whitefish.' Total registered population approximately 200. Dakelh ethnic group.

Kwakiutl (Fort Rupert)

Eight reserves near the north end of Vancouver Island. The Kwakiutl are also known as the Fort Rupert Band and were formerly known as the Kwawkewlth Band, which itself was formed from a merger of three bands in 1964 and subsequently divided in 1981. Total registered population approximately 600. Kwakwaka'wakw ethnic group.

Kwantlen (Langley)

Six reserves near Langley in the Fraser Valley. Formerly known as the Langley Band. Total registered population approximately 200. Halq'emeylem ethnic group.

Kwa-Wa-Aineuk

Ten reserves on northern Vancouver Island. Total registered population less than 100.

Kwaw Kwaw A Pilt

Two reserves near Chilliwack. The nation was formed in 1979. Total registered population approximately 100. Halq'emeylem ethnic group.

Kwayhquitlim (Coquitlam)

Two reserves east of Vancouver, near the Coquitlam River. The nation was established in 1979. Total registered population approximately 100. Halq'emeylem ethnic group.

Kwiakah

Two reserves near Campbell River. Total registered population less than 100. Kwakwaka'wakw ethnic group.

Kwicksutaineuk-Ah-Kwaw-Ah-Mish

Twelve reserves on southern Vancouver Island. Total registered population approximately 300.

Kyuquot. See *Ka:'yu:'K't'h'/Che:K'tles7et'h'*

Lakahahmen

Ten reserves near Deroche in the Fraser Valley. Total registered population approximately 300. Halq'emeylem ethnic group.

Lakalzap (Greenville)

Three reserves in northern British Columbia, near the Nass River. Sometimes spelled Laxqalts'ap. Total registered population approximately 1,500. Nisga'a ethnic group.

Lake Babine. See *Nat'oot'en*

Langley. See *Kwantlen*

Lax Kw'aalams

Seventy-two reserves on the north mainland coast. Total registered population approximately 2,400. Tsimshian ethnic group.

Lheidli T'enneh (Lheit-Lit'en/Fort George)

Five reserves in central British Columbia, near Prince George. Formerly known as the Fort George Band, the nation became Lheit-Lit'en, by which name it is sometimes still known. The name translates as 'people from where the rivers meet.' Total registered population approximately 300.

Lillooet

Seven reserves near Lillooet. Formerly part of the Fraser River Band. Total registered population approximately 300. Stl'atl'imx ethnic group.

Little Shuswap

Five reserves in the southern interior, near Chase. Total registered population approximately 300. Secwepemc ethnic group.

Lower Kootenay

Nine reserves in southeastern British Columbia, near Creston. Total registered population approximately 200. Ktunaxa ethnic group.

Lower Nicola

Ten reserves in the Nicola Valley, near Merritt. Total registered population approximately 800. Nlaka'pamux ethnic group.

Lower Similkameen

Eleven reserves near Keremeos. Total registered population approximately 400. Okanagan ethnic group.

Lyackson

Three reserves on Valdes Island, off the east coast of Vancouver Island. Total registered population approximately 200. Hul'qumi'num ethnic group.

Lytton

Fifty-four reserves near the confluence of the Fraser and Thompson rivers. Total registered population approximately 1,500. Nlaka'pamux ethnic group.

McLeod Lake

Five reserves in northern British Columbia, near McLeod Lake. Total registered population approximately 400. Sekani ethnic group.

Malahat

Two reserves on southern Vancouver Island. The Malahat are one of five bands, along with Pauquachin, Tsartlip, Tsawout, and Tseycum, created by the 1957 split of the Saanich Tribe. Total registered population approximately 200. Hul'qumi'num ethnic group.

Mamaleleqala Qwe'Qwa'Sot'Enox

Three reserves on the central mainland coast. Formerly known as Mamalillikulla. Total registered population approximately 300. Kwakwaka'wakw ethnic group.

Masset. See *Old Masset Village Council*

Matsqui

Four reserves in the central Fraser Valley. In the Halkomelem language Matsqui means 'easy portage' or 'easy travelling.' Total registered population approximately 200. Halq'emeylem ethnic group.

Metlakatla

Sixteen reserves on the north mainland coast, near Prince Rupert. Name may be translated as 'a passage connecting two bodies of salt water.' Total registered population approximately 600. Tsimshian ethnic group.

Moricetown

Seven reserves in north-central British Columbia. Named

after Father Adrien Morice. Total population approximately 1,400. Wet'suwet'en ethnic group.

Mount Currie (Pemberton)
Ten reserves near Pemberton. Total registered population approximately 1,500. Sometimes regarded as Stl'atl'imx and sometimes as Lil'wet'ul.

Mowachaht
Seventeen reserves on the west coast of Vancouver Island. Formerly known as the Nootka Band. The Mowachaht and the Muchalaht amalgamated in the 1950s, retaining the name Mowachaht. Total registered population approximately 400. Nuu'chah'nulth ethnic group.

Musqueam (X'muzk'i'um)
Four reserves near Vancouver. Name translates from the Halkomelem language as 'place always to get iris-like plant.' Total registered population approximately 900. Halq'emeylem ethnic group.

Nadleh Whut'en (Fraser Lake)
Seven reserves in north-central British Columbia, near Fraser Lake. Formerly known as Fraser Lake, the band changed its name in 1990. Total registered population approximately 400. Dakelh ethnic group.

Nak'azdli (Necoslie)
Nineteen reserves in north-central British Columbia, near Fort St James. The band changed its name from Necoslie to Nak'azdli in 1989. Either version may be translated as 'when arrows were flying.' Total registered population approximately 1,300. Dakelh ethnic group.

Namgis (Nimpkish)
Eight reserves near Alert Bay. Formerly known as Nimpkish, the nation is named for a mythical sea monster. Total registered population approximately 1,400. Kwakwaka'wakw ethnic group.

Nanaimo (Sne ney mux)
Six reserves near Nanaimo and Gabriola Island. Name

translates as 'people of many names' or as 'big strong tribe.' Total registered population approximately 1,200. Hul'qumi'num ethnic group.

Nanoose

One reserve on the east coast of Vancouver Island. Total registered population approximately 200. Hul'qumi'num ethnic group.

Nat'oot'en (Lake Babine)

Twenty-four reserves in central British Columbia, near Babine Lake. Total registered population approximately 1,600. Sometimes considered part of Dakelh ethnic group.

Nazko

Nineteen reserves in central British Columbia. Total registered population approximately 300. Dakelh ethnic group.

Necoslie. See *Nak'azdli*

Nee-Tahi-Buhn (Omineca)

Eleven reserves in central British Columbia, west of Prince George. In 1984 the Omineca split into two bands, Broman Lake and the Nee-Tahi-Buhn. Total registered population approximately 200. Wet'suwet'en ethnic group.

Nemiah Valley. See *Xeni Gwet'in*

Neskonlith

Three reserves in south-central British Columbia, near Chase. Total registered population approximately 500. Secwepemc ethnic group.

New Westminster

One reserve on Poplar Island in the lower Fraser River, near New Westminster. Total registered population less than 100. Halq'emeylem ethnic group.

Nicomen

Sixteen reserves in south-central British Columbia. Total registered population approximately 100. Nlaka'pamux ethnic group.

Nimpkish. See *Namgis*

Nitinaht. See *Ditidaht*

Nooaitch

Two reserves in south-central British Columbia. Total registered population approximately 200. Nlaka'pamux ethnic group.

North Thompson

Five reserves in south-central British Columbia, near Barrière. Total registered population approximately 500. Secwepemc ethnic group.

Nuchatlaht

Eleven reserves on the northwest coast of Vancouver Island. Total registered population approximately 200. Nuu'chah'nulth ethnic group.

Nuwitti. See *Tlatlasikwala*

Nuxalk (Bella Coola)

Seven reserves on the central mainland coast. Formerly known as the Bella Coola. Total registered population approximately 1,200.

Ohamil. See *Shxw'ow'hamel*

Ohiaht. See *Huu-ay-aht*

Okanagan

Six reserves in the Okanagan, near Vernon. Total registered population approximately 1,400.

Old Masset Village Council (Masset)

Twenty-six reserves on Haida Gwaii (Queen Charlotte Islands). Formerly known as the Masset Band. Total registered population approximately 2,200. Haida ethnic group.

Omineca. See *Broman Lake* and *Nee-Tahi-Buhn*

Opetchesaht

Five reserves near Port Alberni in central Vancouver Island. Total registered population approximately 200. Nuu'chah'nulth ethnic group.

Oregon Jack Creek

Six reserves in south-central British Columbia. Total registered population approximately 100. Nlaka'pamux ethnic group.

Osoyoos

Two reserves near Osoyoos. Name derives from Okanagan word for a strip of land dividing Osoyoos Lake. Total registered population approximately 400. Okanagan ethnic group.

Oweekeno

Three reserves on the central mainland coast. Possible translations of Oweekeno include 'portage makers' and 'right-minded people.' Total registered population approximately 200.

Pacheenaht

Four reserves on Vancouver Island, near Port Renfrew. Total registered population approximately 200. Nuu'chah'nulth ethnic group.

Pauquachin

Three reserves on southwestern Vancouver Island. One of five bands, along with Malahat, Tsartlip, Tsawout, and Tseycum, created by the 1957 subdivision of the Saanich Tribe. Total registered population approximately 300. Straits Salish ethnic group.

Pavilion. See Ts'kw'aylaxw

Pemberton. See Mount Currie

Penelakut

Four reserves on the Gulf Islands in southern British Columbia. Penelakut translates as 'something buried.' Total registered population approximately 700. Hul'qumi'num ethnic group.

Penticton

Four reserves near Penticton. Total registered population approximately 700. Okanagan ethnic group.

Peters

Three reserves in the upper Fraser Valley. Formerly known as the Squawits Band and once part of the Tait Band. Total registered population approximately 100. Halq'emeylem ethnic group.

Popkum

Two reserves in the upper Fraser Valley. Formerly part of the Tait Band. Total registered population less than 100. Halq'emeylem ethnic group.

Prophet River

One reserve in northeastern British Columbia. Split away from the Fort Nelson Band (formerly known as the Slave Indian Band) in 1974. Total registered population approximately 200. Dene-thah, Dunne-za, and Sekani ethnic groups.

Qualicum

One reserve on the east coast of Vancouver Island. Name translates as 'place of dog salmon'. Total registered population approximately 100. Kwakwaka'wakw ethnic group.

Quatsino

Nineteen reserves on northeastern Vancouver Island, near Quatsino Sound. Possible translations include 'people of the north country' and 'downstream people'. Total registered population approximately 400. Kwakwaka'wakw ethnic group.

Red Bluff (Quesnel)

Four reserves in central British Columbia, near Quesnel. Formerly known as the Quesnel Band. Total registered population approximately 100. Dakelh ethnic group.

Sai Kuz Carrier. See *Stony Creek*

St Mary's

Five reserves in southeastern British Columbia. Total registered population approximately 300. Ktunaxa ethnic group.

Samahquam

Five reserves near the Lillooet River. Total registered population approximately 300. Stl'atl'imx ethnic group.

Saulteau

One reserve in northeastern British Columbia, near Moberly Lake. Total registered population approximately 600. Not associated with any of the major ethnic groups of British Columbia, as the ancestors of the Saulteau people appear to have first settled in the province in the mid- to late nineteenth century.

Scowlitz

Three reserves in the Fraser Valley. Formerly part of the Harrison River Band. Total registered population approximately 200. Halq'emeylem ethnic group.

Seabird Island

One reserve on Seabird Island in the Fraser River. Total registered population approximately 600. Halq'emeylem ethnic group.

Sechelt

Thirty-three 'band lands' near Sechelt on the south mainland coast, north of Vancouver. 'Sechelt' may be the word the people called themselves, although it has also been suggested that it is derived from a native word meaning 'to climb' or from the English 'sea shelter.' Total registered population approximately 900.

Semiahmoo

One reserve on the southwest mainland, south of Vancouver. Total registered population approximately 100. Halq'emeylem ethnic group.

Seton Lake

Seven reserves in south-central British Columbia, near Shalalth. Total registered population approximately 600. Stl'atl'imx ethnic group.

Shackan

Two reserves in the Nicola Valley. Total registered population approximately 200. Nlaka'pamux ethnic group.

Sheshaht

Eight reserves on central Vancouver Island, near Port Alberni. Total registered population approximately 800.

Shuswap

Two reserves in southern British Columbia, near Invermere. Total registered population approximately 300.

Shxw'ow'hamel (Ohamil)

Three reserves in the upper Fraser Valley, near Laidlaw. Total registered population approximately 100. Halq'emeylem ethnic group.

Sikokoak (Glen Vowell)

One reserve near the Skeena River in northwestern British Columbia. Total registered population approximately 300. Gitxsan ethnic group.

Siska

Eleven reserves in southern British Columbia, near Lytton. Total registered population approximately 300. Nlaka'pamux ethnic group.

Skawahlook

Two reserves in the upper Fraser Valley. Total registered population approximately 100. Halq'emeylem ethnic group.

Skeetchestn (Deadman's Creek)

One reserve in south-central British Columbia, near Savona. Formerly known as Deadman's Creek. Total registered population approximately 400. Secwepemc ethnic group.

Skidegate

Eleven reserves on Haida Gwaii (Queen Charlotte Islands). Skidegate translates as 'red paint stone' and was the hereditary name of one of the chiefs. Total registered population approximately 1,500. Haida ethnic group.

Skookum Chuck

Ten reserves near the Lillooet River. Translates as 'turbulent river.' Total registered population approximately 300. Stl'atl'imx ethnic group.

Skowkale

Two reserves in the Fraser Valley. Formerly known as the Skulkayn Band. Total registered population approximately 200. Halq'emeylem ethnic group.

Skuppah

Eight reserves in southern British Columbia, near Lytton. Total registered population approximately 100. Nlaka'pamux ethnic group.

Skwah

Five reserves near Chilliwack. Formerly part of the Chilliwack Band. Total registered population approximately 400. Halq'emeylem ethnic group.

Skway

Two reserves near Chilliwack. Formerly part of the Chilliwack Band. Total registered population approximately 200. Halq'emeylem ethnic group.

Sliammon

Six reserves near Powell River. Total registered population approximately 800.

Sne ney mux. See *Nanaimo*

Soda Creek

Two reserves in central British Columbia, near Williams Lake. The name is derived from the white alkali that dries on rocks nearby. Total registered population approximately 300. Secwepemc ethnic group.

Songhees

Four reserves on southern Vancouver Island. Possibly translates as 'people gathered from scattered places.' Total registered population approximately 400. Straits Salish ethnic group.

Sooke. See *T'Sou-ke*

Soowahlie

One reserve in the Fraser Valley, near the Chilliwack River. Total registered population approximately 300. Halq'emeylem ethnic group.

Spallumcheen

Three reserves in the southern interior, near Enderby. Total registered population approximately 600. Secwepemc ethnic group.

Spuzzum

Sixteen reserves near the Fraser Canyon in southern British

Columbia. Total registered population approximately 200.
Nlaka'pamux ethnic group.

Squamish

Twenty-five reserves north of Vancouver, including parts
of the north shore of Burrard Inlet. Total registered population approximately 2,600.

Squiala

Three reserves in the Fraser Valley. Formerly part of the
Chilliwack Band. Total registered population approximately 200. Halq'emeylem ethnic group.

Stellat'en (Stellaquo)

Two reserves in central British Columbia, west of Prince
George. Name from two words meaning 'river' and 'pe-
ninsula.' Total registered population approximately 300.
Dakelh ethnic group.

Stone

Five reserves in central British Columbia, near Williams
Lake. Total registered population approximately 300.
Tsilhqot'in ethnic group.

Stony Creek (Sai Kuz Carrier)

Ten reserves in central British Columbia, near Stony Creek.
Total registered population approximately 700. Dakelh ethnic group.

Stuart-Trembleur Lake. See *Tl'azt'en*

Sumas

Two reserves in the Fraser Valley. Sumas translates as 'big
flat opening.' Total registered population approximately
300. Halq'emeylem ethnic group.

Tahltan

Eleven reserves in northwestern British Columbia, near Telegraph Creek. Total registered population approximately
1,300.

Takla Lake

Eighteen reserves in central British Columbia. The North
Takla Lake and Fort Connelly bands amalgamated in the

late 1950s, forming the Takla Lake Band. Takla possibly means 'at the end of the lake.' Total registered population approximately 500. Dakelh ethnic group.

Taku River Tlingit
Located in northwestern British Columbia, near Atlin. The traditional territory of the Taku River Tlingit extends into the southern Yukon and Alaska.

Tanakteuk
Seven reserves on the central mainland coast. Total registered population approximately 200. Kwakwaka'wakw ethnic group.

Tla-o-qui-aht (Clayoquot)
Ten reserves near Tofino, on the west coast of Vancouver Island. Formerly known as Clayoquot. Tla-o-qui-aht translates as 'people of other tribes.' Total registered population approximately 600. Nuu'chah'nulth ethnic group.

Tlatlasikwala (Nuwitti)
Six reserves near Alert Bay. Changed name from the Nuwitti Band in 1985. Total registered population less than 100. Kwakwaka'wakw ethnic group.

Tl'azt'en (Stuart-Trembleur Lake)
Nineteen reserves in north-central British Columbia, near Stuart Lake. Formerly known as the Stuart-Trembleur Lake Band, a name that itself resulted from a late 1950s amalgamation of five bands. Tl'azt'en means 'people by the edge of the bay.' Total registered population approximately 1,300. Dakelh ethnic group.

Tl'etinqox. See *Anaham*

Tlowitsis-Mumtagilia (Turnour Island)
Eleven reserves on the central mainland coast. Changed name from Turnour Island Band in 1983. Total registered population approximately 300. Kwakwaka'wakw ethnic group.

Tobacco Plains
Two reserves in southeastern British Columbia, near

Cranbrook. Total registered population approximately 200. Ktunaxa ethnic group.

Toosey

Four reserves in central British Columbia, near Williams Lake. Total registered population approximately 200. Tsilhqot'in ethnic group.

Toquaht

Seven reserves on the west coast of Vancouver Island. Total population approximately 200. Nuu'chah'nulth ethnic group.

Tsartlip

Four reserves on the Gulf Islands and near Saanich. One of five bands, along with Malahat, Pauquachin, Tsawout, and Tseycum, created by the 1957 subdivision of the Saanich Tribe. Total registered population approximately 700. Straits Salish ethnic group.

Tsawataineuk (Kingcome Inlet)

Five reserves on the central mainland coast. Also known as Kingcome Inlet. Total registered population approximately 500. Kwakwaka'wakw ethnic group.

Tsawout

Six reserves on the Gulf Islands and near Saanich. One of five bands, along with Malahat, Pauquachin, Tsartlip, and Tseycum, created by the 1957 subdivision of the Saanich Tribe. Total registered population approximately 600. Straits Salish ethnic group.

Tsawwassen

One reserve in southwestern British Columbia. Name translates as 'beach at the mouth' or 'facing the sea.' Total registered population approximately 200. Halq'emeylem ethnic group.

Tsay Keh Dene (Ingenika)

Five reserves in northern British Columbia, near Finlay River. Formerly known as the Ingenika Band and once part of the Finlay River Band, which itself was an amalgamation of the Fort Graham and Fort Ware bands. Tsay Keh Dene translates as 'people of the mountains.' Total registered population approximately 300. Sekani ethnic group.

Tseshaht
. Eight reserves in central Vancouver Island, near Port Alberni. Total registered population approximately 900. Nuu'chah'nulth ethnic group.

Tseycum
Five reserves on the Gulf Islands and near Saanich. One of five bands, along with Malahat, Pauquachin, Tsartlip, and Tsawout, created by the 1957 subdivision of the Saanich Tribe. Total registered population approximately 200. Straits Salish ethnic group.

Ts'kw'aylaxw (Pavilion)
Seven reserves between Lillooet and Cache Creek. Total registered population approximately 500. Stl'atl'imx and Secwepemc ethnic groups.

Tsleil Waututh (Burrard)
Three reserves north of Burrard Inlet in southwestern British Columbia. 'Tsleiliwaututh' is a Halkomelem word meaning 'people of the inlet.' Total registered population approximately 400.

T'Sou-ke (Sooke)
Two reserves on southern Vancouver Island. Total registered population approximately 200. Straits Salish ethnic group.

Tsulquate. See *Gwa'sala-Nakwaxda'xw*
Turnour Island. See *Tlowitsis-Mumtagilia*
Tzeachten
One reserve in the Fraser Valley. Established in the late 1960s. Total registered population approximately 300. Halq'emeylem ethnic group.

Uchucklesaht
Two reserves on southern Vancouver Island. Name may be

translated as 'inside the bay'. Total registered population approximately 200. Nuu'chah'nulth ethnic group.

Ucluelet

Nine reserves on the west coast of Vancouver Island, near Ucluelet. Total registered population approximately 600. Nuu'chah'nulth ethnic group.

Ulkatcho

Nineteen reserves in central British Columbia, near Anahim Lake. Total registered population approximately 700. Dakelh ethnic group.

Union Bar

Seven reserves near the Fraser River, north of Hope. Formerly part of the Tait Band. Total registered population approximately 100. Halq'emeylem ethnic group.

Upper Nicola

Eight reserves in the Nicola Valley, near Merritt. Nicola derives from Nicholas, which was the English name given to a chief by early fur traders. Total registered population approximately 800. Okanagan ethnic group.

Upper Similkameen

Seven reserves near Keremeos. The Upper Similkameen split from the Similkameen in the 1960s. Total registered population approximately 100. Okanagan ethnic group.

Westbank

Three reserves near Kelowna. Total registered population approximately 500. Okanagan ethnic group.

West Moberly

One reserve in northeastern British Columbia, at the west end of Moberly Lake. Formed in 1977 with the split of the Hudson Hope band into the Halfway River and West Moberly bands. Total registered population approximately 100. Dunne-za ethnic group.

We Wai Kai (Cape Mudge)

Five reserves on Vancouver Island, near Campbell River.

Total registered population approximately 800. Kwakwaka'wakw ethnic group.

We Wai kum, Kwiakah (Campbell River)
Five reserves on the east coast of Vancouver Island, near Campbell River. Formerly known as the Campbell River Band. Total registered population approximately 500. Kwakwaka'wakw ethnic group.

Whispering Pines (Clinton)
Three reserves in south-central British Columbia. Formerly known as the Clinton Band. Total registered population approximately 100. Secwepemc ethnic group.

Williams Lake
Eight reserves in central British Columbia, near Williams Lake. Named after Chief William. Total registered population approximately 400. Secwepemc ethnic group.

Xaxli'p (Fountain)
Seventeen reserves near Lillooet. Total registered population approximately 700. Stl'atl'imx ethnic group.

Xeni Gwet'in (Nemiah Valley)
Eight reserves in central British Columbia, near Chilco Lake. Total registered population approximately 400. Tsilhqot'in ethnic group.

X'muzk'i'um. See *Musqueam*

Yakweakwioose
One reserve in the Fraser Valley. Total registered population approximately 100. Halq'emeylem ethnic group.

Yale
Eighteen reserves near Yale, in the lower Fraser Canyon. Total registered population approximately 200. Halq'emeylem ethnic group.

Yekooche (Yekootchet'en)
Located in central British Columbia, near Fort St James. Total registered population approximately 200. Dakelh ethnic group.

Major Ethnic Groups

There is no consensus on either the distinction of major ethnic groups among First Nations in British Columbia or the specific nations that belong to the larger ethnic groups. Some nations constitute ethnic groups in and of themselves. The nature and identification of ethnic groups is subject to ongoing research and debate.

Champagne and Aishihik
> Traditional territories are mostly in the Yukon but extend into the northwest corner of British Columbia.

Comox
> Traditional territories are on the central east coast of Vancouver Island. Has sometimes been considered part of the Kwakwaka'wakw.

Dakelh
> Formerly known as Carrier. Traditional territories are in central British Columbia. Member nations are Alexandria, Burns Lake, Cheslatta, Kluskus, Lheidli T'enneh, Nadleh Whut'en, Nak'azdli, Nazko, Red Bluff, Stellat'en, Stony Creek, Takla Lake, Tl'azt'en, Ulkatcho, and Yekooche.

Dene-thah
> Formerly known as Slave or Slavey. Traditional territories are in northeastern British Columbia. Many of the nations in this part of the province represent a mixture of Dene-thah, Dunne-za, and Sekani ethnic origins. These nations are Blueberry River, Doig River, Fort Nelson, Fort Ware, Halfway River, McLeod Lake, Prophet River, Tsay Keh Dene, and West Moberly.

Dunne-za
> Formerly known as Beaver. Traditional territories are in northeastern British Columbia. Many of the nations in this

part of the province represent a mixture of Dene-thah, Dunne-za, and Sekani ethnic origins. These nations are Blueberry River, Doig River, Fort Nelson, Fort Ware, Halfway River, McLeod Lake, Prophet River, Tsay Keh Dene, and West Moberly.

Ditidaht. See *Nuu'chah'nulth*

Gitxsan
Traditional territories are in northwestern British Columbia, around the Skeena River. Member nations are Gitanmaax, Gitanyow, Gitsegukla, Gitwangak, Kispiox, and Sikokoak.

Haida
Traditional territories encompass Haida Gwaii (Queen Charlotte Islands). Member nations are Old Masset Village Council, formerly known as Masset, and Skidegate.

Haisla
Also known as Kitimat and Kitamaat. Traditional territories are on the central mainland coast.

Halq'emeylem (including Sto:lo, Musqueam, and Tsawwassen)
Traditional territories are in southeastern British Columbia. Member nations are Chehalis, Katzie, Kwayhquitlim, Musqueam, New Westminster, Semiahmoo, Shxw'ow'hamel, Tsawwassen, and Yale. The Halq'emeylem also includes nations commonly associated with Sto:lo: Aitchelitz, Chawathil, Cheam, Kwantlen, Kwaw Kwaw A Pilt, Lakahahmen, Matsqui, Peters, Popkum, Scowlitz, Seabird Island, Shxw'ow'hamel, Skawahlook, Skowkale, Skwah, Skway, Soowahlie, Squiala, Sumas, Tzeachten, Union Bar, and Yakweakwioose.

Heiltsuk
Formerly known as the Bella Bella. Traditional territories are on central mainland coast.

Homalco
Traditional territories are around Bute Inlet on the south-central mainland coast. The Homalco have sometimes been judged to be part of the Kwakwaka'wakw.

Hul'qumi'num
Traditional territories are north of the Straits Salish on southeastern Vancouver Island. Member nations are Chemainus, Cowichan, Cowichan Lake, Halalt, Lyackson, Malahat, Nanaimo, Nanoose, and Penelakut.

Kaska
Traditional territories are in northern British Columbia and the Yukon. The member nation in British Columbia is Dease River.

Klahoose
Traditional territories are around Cortez Island and the adjacent mainland area of the south-central coast. The Klahoose have sometimes been seen as part of the Kwakwaka'wakw.

Ktunaxa
Formerly known as Kootenay and Kutenai. Traditional territories are in southeastern British Columbia. Member nations are Columbia Lake, Lower Kootenay, St Mary's, and Tobacco Plains.

Kwakwaka'wakw
Formerly known as Kwakiutl and Kwagiulth. Traditional territories cover northeastern Vancouver Island and the adjacent mainland. Member nations are Gwa'sala-Nakwaxda'xw, Kwakiutl, Kwiakah, Mamaleleqala Qwe'Qwa'Sot'Enox, Namgis, Qualicum, Quatsino, Tanakteuk, Tlatlasikwala, Tlowitsis-Mumtagilia, Tsawataineuk, We Wai Kai, and We Wai kum, Kwiakah. The Comox, Homalco, and Klahoose nations have sometimes been regarded as part of the Kwakwaka'wakw.

Lil'wet'ul. See *Stl'atl'imx.*

Nat'oot'en
Formerly known as Babine and Lake Babine. Traditional territories are in north-central British Columbia. Sometimes considered part of Dakelh.

Nisga'a
Formerly known as Niska and Nishga. Traditional territories

are in the area of the Nass River in northwestern British Columbia. Member nations are Gitlakdamix, Gitwinksihlkw, Kincolith, and Lakalzap.

Nlaka'pamux

Formerly known as Thompson. Traditional territories are in the southern interior of the province. Member nations are Ashcroft, Boothroyd, Boston Bar, Cook's Ferry, Kanaka Bar, Lytton, Nicomen, Oregon Jack Creek, Siska, Skuppah, and Spuzzum. Four nations of the Nicola Valley – Coldwater, Lower Nicola, Nooaitch, and Shackan – are sometimes viewed as part of the Nlaka'pamux.

Nuu'chah'nulth

Formerly known as Nootka. Traditional territories are on the west coast of Vancouver Island. Member nations are Ahousaht, Ehattesaht, Hesquiaht, Huu-ay-aht, Ka:'yu:'K't'h'/ Che:K'tles7et'h', Mowachaht, Muchalaht, Nuchatlaht, Opetchesaht, Opitsaht, Tla-o-qui-aht, Toquaht, Tseshaht, Uchucklesaht, and Ucluelet. The Pacheenaht and Ditidaht are sometimes considered distinct and sometimes as member nations of the Nuu'chah'nulth.

Nuxalk

Formerly known as Bella Coola. Traditional territories are on the central mainland coast.

Okanagan

Traditional territories are in the Okanagan region of south-central British Columbia. Member nations are Lower Similkameen, Okanagan, Osoyoos, Penticton, Upper Similkameen, and Westbank. The Upper Nicola First Nations are sometimes considered Okanagan.

Oweekeno

Traditional territories are on the central mainland coast.

Pacheenaht. See *Nuu'chah'nulth*

Sechelt

Also known as Shishalh. Traditional territories are around Sechelt on the Sunshine Coast.

Secwepemc

Formerly known as Shuswap. Traditional territories are in the southern interior of the province. Member nations are Adams Lake, Bonaparte, Canim Lake, Canoe Creek, Dog Creek, Esketemc, High Bar, Kamloops, Little Shuswap, Neskonlith, North Thompson, Skeetchestn, Soda Creek, Spallumcheen, Ts'kw'aylaxw, Whispering Pines, and Williams Lake.

Sekani

Traditional territories are in northeastern British Columbia. Many of the nations in this part of the province have a mixture of Dene-thah, Dunne-za, and Sekani ethnic origins, including Blueberry River, Doig River, Fort Nelson, Fort Ware, Halfway River, McLeod Lake, Prophet River, Tsay Keh Dene, and West Moberly.

Sliammon

Traditional territories are around Powell River on the south-central mainland coast.

Squamish

Traditional territories are in southeastern British Columbia, extending from Vancouver to Pemberton and encompassing Howe Sound.

Stl'atl'imx

Formerly known as Lillooet. Traditional territories are in the southern interior of the province. Member nations are Anderson Lake, Bridge River, Cayoose Creek, Douglas, Lillooet, Samahquam, Seton Lake, Skookum Chuck, Ts'kw'aylaxw, and Xaxli'p. Mount Currie is sometimes regarded as Stl'atl'imx and sometimes as a distinct group known as Lil'wet'ul.

Straits Salish

Traditional territories are on southeastern Vancouver Island and parts of the Gulf Islands. Member nations are Beecher Bay, Esquimalt, Lekwammen, Pauquachin, Songhees, Tsartlip, Tsawout, Tseycum, and T'Sou-ke.

Tahltan

Traditional territories are in northwestern British Columbia. The Iskut First Nation is often deemed to be Tahltan.

Taku Tlingit

Formerly known as Inland Tlingit. Traditional territories are in northwestern British Columbia.

Tsilhqot'in

Formerly known as Chilcotin. Traditional territories are in the Chilcotin area in south-central British Columbia. Member nations are Alexis Creek, Anaham, Stone, Toosey, and Xeni Gwet'in.

Tsimshian

Traditional territories are on the north mainland coast. Member nations are Git'k'a'ata, Kitasoo, Kitkatla, Kitselas, Kitsumkalum, Lax Kw'aalams, and Metlakatla.

Tsleil Waututh

Formerly known as Burrard. Traditional territories are around the north shores of Burrard Inlet and Indian Arm on the southeast mainland.

Wet'suwet'en

Sometimes considered part of the Dakelh (Carrier). Traditional territories are in west-central British Columbia. Member nations are Broman Lake, Hagwilget, Moricetown, and Nee-Tahi-Buhn.

Appendix 3
Excerpts from the Royal Proclamation, 1763

By the King, a Royal Proclamation

Whereas We have taken into Our Royal Consideration the extensive and valuable Acquisitions in America, secured to our Crown by the late Definitive Treaty of Peace, concluded at Paris, the 10th Day of February last; and being desirous that all Our loving Subjects, as well of our Kingdom as of our Colonies in America, may avail themselves with all convenient Speed, of the great Benefits and Advantages which must accrue therefrom to the Commerce, Manufacturers, and Navigation, We have thought fit, with the Advice of our Privy Council, to issue this our Royal Proclamation ...

And whereas it is just and reasonable, and essential to our Interest, and the Security of our Colonies, that the several Nations or Tribes of Indians with whom We are connected, and who live under our Protection, should not be molested or disturbed in the Possession of such Parts of Our Dominion and Territories as, not having been ceded to or purchased by Us, are reserved to them, or any of them, as their Hunting Grounds ...

And We do further declare it to be Our Royal Will and Pleasure, for the present as aforesaid, to reserve under our sovereignty, Protection, and Dominion, for the use of the said Indians, all the Lands and Territories not included within the Limits of Our said Three new Governments, or within the Limits of the Territory granted to the Hudson's Bay Company, as also all the Lands and Territories lying to the Westward of the Sources of the Rivers which fall into the Sea from the West and North West as aforesaid.

And We do hereby strictly forbid, on Pain of our Displeasure, all our loving Subjects from making any Purchases or Settlements whatever, or taking Possession of any Lands above reserved, without our especial leave and Licence for that Purpose first obtained. And we do further strictly enjoin and require all Persons whatever who have either wilfully or inadvertently seated themselves upon any Lands within the Countries above described, or upon any other Lands which, not having been ceded to or purchased by Us, are still reserved to the said Indians as aforesaid, forthwith to remove themselves from such settlements.

And whereas great Frauds and Abuses have been committed in purchasing Lands of the Indians, to the great Prejudice of our Interests, and to the great Dissatisfaction of the said Indians; In order, therefore, to prevent such Irregularities for the future, and to the end that the Indians may be convinced of our Justice and determined Resolution to remove all reasonable Cause of Discontent, We do, with the Advice of our Privy Council strictly enjoin and require, that no private Person do presume to make any purchases from the said Indians, within those parts of our Colonies where, We have thought Proper to allow Settlement; but that, if at any Time any of the Said Indians should be inclined to dispose of the said Lands, the same shall be Purchased only for Us, in our Name, at some public Meeting or Assembly of the said Indians, to be held for the Purpose by the Governor or Commander in Chief of our Colony respectively within which they shall lie ...

Given at our Court at St. James the 7th Day of October 1763, in the Third Year of our Reign.

God Save the King

Excerpts from the Laurier Memorial, 1910

To Sir Wilfrid Laurier, Premier of the Dominion of Canada

From the Chiefs of the Shuswap, Okanagan and Couteau Tribes of British Columbia

Presented at Kamloops, B.C., August 25, 1910

Dear Sir and Father

We take this opportunity of your visiting Kamloops to speak a few words to you. We welcome you here, and we are glad we have met you in our country. We want you to be interested in us, and to understand more fully the conditions under which we live ... We speak to you the more freely because you are a member of the white race with whom we first became acquainted, and which we call in our tongue 'real whites.'

One hundred years next year they came amongst us here at Kamloops and erected a trading post. After other whites came to this country in 1858 we differentiated them from the first whites as their manners were so much different, and we applied the term 'real whites' to the latter (viz., the fur traders of the Northwest and Hudson [*sic*] Bay companies) ... The 'real whites' we found were good people. We could depend on their word, and we trusted and respected them. They did not interfere with us nor attempt to break up our tribal organizations, laws, and customs. They did not try to force their conceptions of things to us to our harm. Nor did they stop us from catching fish, hunting, etc. ... They never tried to steal or appropriate our country, nor take food and life from us. They acknowledged our ownership of the country, and treated our Chiefs as men ...

When they first came amongst us there were only Indians here. They found the people of each tribe supreme in their own territory, and having tribal boundaries known and recognized by all ...

Just 52 years ago the other whites came to this country. They found us just the same as the first or 'real whites' had found us, only we had larger bands of horses, had some cattle, and in many places we cultivated the land. They found us happy, healthy, strong and numerous ... We were friendly and helped these whites also, for had we not learned the first whites had done us no harm? Only when some of them killed us we revenged on them. Then we thought there are some bad ones among them, but surely on the whole they must be good ... At first they looked only for gold. We knew the latter was our property, but as we did not use it much nor need it to live by we did not object to their searching for it. They told us, 'Your country is rich and you will be made wealthy by our coming. We wish just to pass over your lands in quest for gold.' Soon they saw the country was good, and some of them made up their mind, to settle it. They commenced to take up pieces of land here and there ...

The whites made a government in Victoria – perhaps the Queen made it ... At this time they did not deny the Indian tribes owned the whole country and everything in it. They told us we did ...

... Gradually as the whites of this country became more and more powerful, and we less and less powerful, they little by little changed their policy towards us, and commenced to put restrictions on us. Their government or chiefs have taken every advantage of our friendliness, weakness and ignorance to impose on us in every way ...

After time when they saw that our patience might get exhausted and that we might cause trouble if we thought all the land was to be occupied by whites they set aside many small reservations for us here and there over the country. This was their proposal not ours, and we never accepted these reservations as settlement for anything ...

In a petition signed by fourteen of our Chiefs and sent to your Indian department, July 1908, we pointed out the disabilities under which we labor owing to the inadequacy of most of the reservations, some having hardly any good land, others no irrigation water, etc., our limitations regarding pasture lands for stock owing to fencing of so-called government lands by whites; the severe restrictions put on us lately by the government regarding hunting and fishing; the depletion of salmon by over fishing of the whites, and other matters affecting us. In many places we are debarred from camping, travelling, gathering roots and obtaining wood and water as heretofore. Our people are fined and imprisoned for breaking the game and fish laws using the same game and fish which we were told would always be ours for food. Gradually we are becoming regarded as trespassers over a large portion of this our country ... We condemn the whole policy of the B.C. government towards the Indian tribes of this country as utterly unjust, shameful and blundering in every way. We denounce same as being the main cause of the unsatisfactory condition of Indian affairs in this country and at animosity and friction with the whites ... We believe it is not the desire nor the policy of your government that these conditions should exist. We demanded that our land question be settled, and ask that treaties be made ... Hoping you have had a pleasant sojourn in this country, and wishing you a good journey home, we remain

Yours very sincerely,

The Chiefs of the Shuswap, Okanagan, and Couteau or Thompson Tribes

– Per their secretary, J.A. Teit

Excerpts from the Nisga'a Agreement-in-Principle, 1996

General Provisions

The Nisga'a will continue to be an aboriginal people under the Constitution Act, 1982.

Nisga'a will continue to be entitled to the rights and benefits of other Canadian Citizens.

Lands owned by the Nisga'a will no longer be reserve lands under the Indian Act.

The Charter of Rights and Freedoms will apply to Nisga'a government and its institutions.

Nisga'a jurisdiction over Nisga'a citizens on Nisga'a land will be phased in over time.

Eventually, the Indian Act will no longer apply to the Nisga'a.

All parties agree that the final agreement will provide certainty with respect to Nisga'a rights, title and obligations.

The Criminal Code of Canada and other laws of general application will continue to apply.

Land and Resources

The Nisga'a will own two types of lands – Nisga'a lands and fee simple lands.

Nisga'a lands

There will be about 1,930 square kilometres of Nisga'a lands in the Lower Nass River area. Nisga'a lands will be communally owned. These lands will include the four Nisga'a villages, New Aiyansh (Gitlakdamiks), Canyon City (Gitwinksihlkw), Greenville (Lakalazap) and Kincolith (Gingolx).

Fifty-six Indian reserves in the area will cease to be Indian reserves and will become Nisga'a lands.

These lands will not include existing fee simple lands, or land subject to agriculture leases and wood lot licences.

The Nisga'a will own both surface resources (including forests) and subsurface resources on Nisga'a lands.

Existing legal interests on Nisga'a lands, such as rights of way, angling and guide outfitter licences and traplines, will continue on their current terms.

Fee Simple Lands
Lands contained within 18 reserves outside of Nisga'a lands will become fee simple lands owned by the Nisga'a government and will be subject to provincial laws. Some of these reserves will increase in size. In total, the increase will not exceed 12.5 square kilometres.

An additional 15 parcels of fee simple land, totalling no more than 2.5 square kilometres, will be owned by the Nisga'a for economic development. These lands will also be subject to provincial laws.

Forest Resources on Nisga'a Lands
After a transitional period, for existing licensees to adjust their operations, the Nisga'a will manage Nisga'a forest resources.

They will be able to implement forest management standards provided these meet or exceed provincial standards, such as the Forest Practices Code.

Protection of Historic Sites and Names of Key Geographic Features
Key cultural sites will be protected through heritage site designation.

Key geographic features will be renamed with Nisga'a names.

Water

The Nisga'a are guaranteed enough water to meet their domestic, industrial and agricultural needs, subject to habitat conservation.

Access

There will be public access to Nisga'a lands for hunting, fishing, and recreation.

Non-Nisga'a residents will have unimpeded access to their lands.

Fisheries

Conservation of fish stocks is the primary consideration.

The Nisga'a will receive an annual treaty-entitlement of salmon, which will, on average, comprise approximately 18 per cent of the Canadian Nass River total allowable catch.

The Nisga'a will be able to sell their salmon.

The Nisga'a will receive an annual entitlement for non-salmon species, such as halibut, oolichan and shellfish. The entitlement will be for domestic purposes and may not be sold.

The Nisga'a will receive $11.5 million towards participation in the coastal commercial fishing industry. This will provide for the purchase of vessels and licences.

The Nisga'a will not establish large fish-processing facilities within 12 years.

Wildlife

The Nisga'a will receive entitlement or hunt moose and other species to be designated.

A wildlife management area will be established, in which the Nisga'a will be entitled to hunt wildlife for domestic purposes, subject to conservation needs.

The Nisga'a will not be able to sell wildlife, but may trade or barter among themselves or with other aboriginal people.

Environmental Assessment and Protection

Environmental protection standards on Nisga'a lands will be set by the Nisga'a. These standards must meet or exceed those set by the federal or provincial government.

Nisga'a Government

Government Structure and Jurisdiction

The Nisga'a will have a Nisga'a government and four village governments, similar to local government structures.

The Nisga'a will adopt a constitution that spells out the structure, duties and membership of their government and ensures it is open and democratic.

The Nisga'a will be able to make laws governing such things as culture and language, employment, public works, regulation of traffic and transportation, land use and solemnization of marriage, among others. The Nisga'a will continue to provide health, child welfare and education services.

People residing on Nisga'a lands who are not Nisga'a citizens: will be consulted about and may seek a review of decisions which directly affect them; and will be able to participate in elected bodies which directly affect them.

Administration of Justice

With the approval of the province:

The Nisga'a government will be able to provide full policing services on their lands as do municipalities. The police must meet provincial standards for training, qualifications and professional standards.

The Nisga'a will be able to establish a Nisga'a court that will have jurisdiction over Nisga'a laws on Nisga'a lands.

Fiscal Financing Agreements

Nisga'a government will receive fiscal transfers to enable them to provide government services at levels generally comparable to those available in the Northwest region of B.C.

The Nisga'a government's ability to raise revenue will be taken into consideration when fiscal transfers are negotiated.

The Nisga'a will receive $190 million which will be paid over a period of years.

Taxation

Nisga'a government will have the power to tax Nisga'a citizens on Nisga'a land.

The Indian tax exemption for Nisga'a citizens will be eliminated after a transitional period of eight years for transaction (i.e. sales) taxes and 12 years for other taxes (i.e. income).

Cultural Artifacts and Heritage Protection

The Royal BC Museum and the Canadian Museum of Civilization will return a significant portion of their collections of Nisga'a artifacts to the Nisga'a. The museums will retain collections of Nisga'a artifacts for the public.

Dispute Resolution

If disputes arise on the application of the treaty, the parties will try to resolve them through cooperation, consultation and mediation. If these efforts fail they will have recourse to arbitration and the BC Supreme Court.

Eligibility and Enrolment

Criteria for Nisga'a enrolment reflect the matrilineal system and the Ayuukhl (traditional law). An enrolment committee comprising eight Nisga'a persons (two from each of the four tribes) is responsible for establishing a register of names. A three-member appeal board will consider appeals from the enrolment committee's decisions.

Ratification of the Agreement-in-Principle

The Nisga'a will ratify the agreement-in-principle in a special assembly of the Nisga'a Nation.

British Columbia and Canada will ratify the agreement-in-principle by signature of the responsible provincial and federal ministers.

Once the agreement-in-principle is ratified by the parties, they will negotiate a final agreement.

First Nations Involved in Treaty Negotiations, January 1998

Affiliated Nations

Cariboo Tribal Council: Affiliated nations include Canim Lake, Canoe Creek, Soda Creek, and Williams Lake

Carrier Sekani Tribal Council: Affiliated nations include Broman Lake, Burns Lake, Nadleh Whut'en, Sai Kuz Carrier (Stony Creek), Stellat'en, Takla Lake, and Tl'azt'en

Champagne-Aishihik: Nations based mostly in the Yukon negotiating a **transboundary agreement**

Council of the Haida Nation: Affiliated nations of Old Masset Village Council and Skidegate

Hul'qumi'num Treaty Group: Affiliated nations of Chemainus, Cowichan, Cowichan Lake, Halalt, Lyackson, and Penelakut

In-SHUCK-ch/N'Quatqua: Affiliated nations of Anderson Lake, Douglas, Samahquam, Skookum Chuck

Kaska Dene Council: Affiliated nations of Dease River, Fort Ware, and Liard River (Yukon) negotiating a transboundary agreement

Ktunaxa Kinbasket Tribal Council: Affiliated nations of Columbia Lake, Lower Kootenay, St Mary's, and Tobacco Plains

Kwakiutl Laich-kwil-Tach Nations Treaty Society: Affiliated nations of Gwa'sala-Nakwaxda'xw, Kwakiutl, Mamaleleqala Qwe'Qwa'Sot'Enox, Tlatlasikwala, Tlowitsis-Mumtagilia, We Wai Kai (Cape Mudge), and We Wai kum, Kwiakah (Campbell River)

Nisga'a: Affiliated nations of Gitlakdamix, Gitwinksihlkw, Kincolith, and Lakalzap

Nuu'chah'nulth Tribal Council: Affiliated nations of Ahousaht, Ehattesaht, Hesquiaht, Huu-ay-aht, Ka:'yu:'K't'h'/Che:K'tles7et'h' (Kyuquot), Mowachaht, Nuchatlaht, Opetchesaht, Tla-o-qui-aht (Clayoquot), Toquaht, Tseshaht, Uchucklesaht, and Ucluelet

Sto:lo Nation: Affiliated nations of Aitchelitz, Chawathil, Cheam, Kwantlen, Kwaw Kwaw A Pilt, Lakahahmen, Matsqui, Popkum, Scowlitz, Seabird Island, Shxw'ow'hamel (Ohamil), Skawahlook, Skowkale, Soowahlie, Squiala, Sumas, Tzeachten, and Yakweakwioose

Te'Mexw Treaty Association: Affiliated nations of Beecher Bay, Malahat, Nanoose, Songhees, and T'Sou-ke (Sooke)

Tsimshian Tribal Council: Affiliated nations of Gitga'at (Git'k'a'ata), Kitasoo, Kitkatla, Kitselas, Kitsumkalum, Lax Kw'aalams, and Metlakatla

Winalagalis: Affiliated nations of Gwa'sala-Nakwaxda'xw, Kwakiutl, Namgis, Quatsino, Tanakteuk, and Tlatlasikwala

Unaffiliated Nations

Cheslatta, Comox, Ditidaht, Esketemc, Gitanyow, Haisla (Kitamaat), Heiltsuk, Homalco, Katzie, Klahoose, Lheit-Lit'en (Lheidli T'enneh), Musqueam, Nanaimo, Nat'oot'en, Nazko, Oweekeno, Pacheenaht, Sechelt, Sliammon, Squamish, Taku River Tlingit, Teslin Tlingit (transboundary agreement), Tsawwassen, Tsay Keh Dene, Ts'kw'aylaxw (Pavilion), Tsleil Waututh (Burrard), Westbank, Xaxli'p (Fountain), Yale, Yekooche

Glossary

Aboriginal people. As defined by the Canadian Constitution, all indigenous people of Canada, including Indians (status and non-status), Métis, and Inuit people.

Aboriginal rights. Rights of aboriginal people, subject to negotiation or adjudication. The Canadian Constitution protects 'aboriginal rights' but fails to state the nature of those rights. Rights may include the freedom to maintain traditional economic and social activities as well as rights to lands, resources, and self-government.

Aboriginal title. Ownership or control of land by aboriginal groups, subject to negotiation or adjudication.

Agreement-in-principle (AIP). The fourth phase of the six-stage treaty negotiation process. The agreement-in-principle outlines the major points of agreement between parties and is meant to form the basis of the treaty.

Anthropology. The study of humans from evolutionary, comparative, and holistic perspectives.

Archaeological site. Any location where there is evidence of past human activity. Locations in British Columbia are rarely designated as archaeological unless they are at least 100 years old.

Archaeology. The branch of anthropology focusing on the activities of humans who lived in the past.

Assembly of First Nations (AFN). Formerly known as the National Indian Brotherhood, the Assembly of First Nations is an organization that promotes the interests of all First Nations in Canada, including aboriginal rights, economic development, education, and health.

Band. As defined in the Indian Act (1989), 'a body of Indians ... for whose use and benefit in common, lands, the legal title to which is vested in Her Majesty, have been set apart.' Many Indian bands now refer to themselves as nations.

Beringia. A large area of land covering portions of north-western North America and northeastern Asia that remained ice free during the last ice age. Most archaeologists believe that Beringia was the first area within the Americas to have been inhabited by people.

Bill C-31. A federal government bill, passed in 1985, that eliminated sexual discrimination in the Indian Act, allowed First Nations to determine who could be a member of the nation, and allowed for the restoration of status for those who had lost it.

Clan. A group of lineages or houses encompassing people who claim descent from a common ancestor, although not all the links between descendants are known.

Community. A band, nation, reserve, or settlement is sometimes referred to as a community.

Comprehensive claim. A claim of aboriginal rights by a First Nation that has not been dealt with by a previous treaty or other legal means. Most comprehensive claims in British Columbia are being negotiated under the BC Treaty Negotiation Commission process.

Constitution, Canadian. The supreme law of Canada. The Constitution includes the Charter of Rights and Freedoms and recognizes aboriginal rights.

Culture. Everything that people learn and share as members of society. Culture includes, but is not limited to, language, values, beliefs, social organization, customs, economic strategies, and technology.

Culture area. A geographic region in which separate societies have similar cultures.

Culture history. A description of cultural change through time.

Cultural resource management (CRM). In British Columbia this usually refers to the identification, assessment, excavation, or protection of archaeological sites that are under threat of destruction by natural or human agency.

Douglas treaties. Fourteen treaties signed by some First Nations on Vancouver Island and Sir James Douglas (representing the interests of the British Crown) between 1850 and 1854. Along with Treaty 8, which was signed by representatives of some First Nations of northeastern British Columbia, these are the only signed treaties in the province.

Enfranchise. Becoming enfranchised involves giving up 'Indian' status to obtain full legal status as a Canadian citizen, including the right to vote.

Ethnic group. People who share the same culture, including language.

Ethnography. Written description of a society based on either the first-hand observation of the writer (the ethnographer) or the memories of individuals.

Ethnology. The study of cultures, often based on ethnographies.

Extinguishment. The cessation of aboriginal rights.

Fiduciary duty. The responsibility or obligation of one party to act in the best interests of another. The Canadian federal government has a fiduciary duty to protect the interests of First Nations.

First Nation. A self-determined organization comprising the descendants of people who lived in what is now British Columbia prior to the arrival of Europeans and Americans in the late eighteenth century.

First Nations Summit. An organization representing those First Nations participating in the BC Treaty Negotiation Commission process.

House. A group of related people, with a recognized chief, who usually lived together in a cedar plank house during the winter months. The house was an important social unit of Northwest Coast peoples prior to colonization.

Indian. One of three groups of aboriginal people recognized in the Constitution (along with Inuit and Métis).

Historically, a term widely used to describe the descendants of the first inhabitants of the Americas.

Indian Act. Document governing relations between First Nations and the federal government.

Indian Band. *See* **Band**

Inuit. One of the three groups of aboriginal people recognized in the Constitution (along with Indians and Métis). Previously known as Eskimos, most Inuit live in northern Canada.

Métis. One of three groups of aboriginal people recognized in the Constitution (along with Indians and Inuit). The Métis are people of mixed aboriginal and French or French-Canadian ancestry.

Modernization. Anthropological term describing the economic, social, political, and religious changes that relate to industrial and technological developments. Modernization usually includes a change in subsistence strategies, an increase in the percentage of the population living in urban areas, and the incorporation of cultural patterns characteristic of Western, industrialized society, such as formal education.

Non-status Indian. A person of aboriginal descent who is not registered with the federal government as a 'registered' or 'status' Indian. Non-status Indians are not governed by the Indian Act and rarely belong to First Nations.

Oral tradition. Information and stories passed orally from generation to generation.

Potlatch. A ceremony to witness events of social significance, such as marriages, the formal assumption of the role of chief, and the attainment or transfer of rights and responsibilities. An important feature of potlatches is the distribution of gifts to guests. Acceptance of the gifts legitimizes the event.

Prehistoric. Before written records. For most of British Columbia the transition from prehistory to history occurs in the late eighteenth and early nineteenth centuries, when Europeans and Americans coming from societies that had writing first encountered First Nations.

Registered Indian. A person whose name appears on a register maintained by the federal government. Registered Indians are governed by the Indian Act.

Reserve. An allotment of land set aside for Indians. There are more than 1,600 reserves in British Columbia. The federal government has jurisdiction over reserves.

Royal Proclamation. Proclaimed in 1763 by King George III to maintain peace and provide a sense of order between British subjects and First Nations. The proclamation essentially asserted that First Nations had rights and established a system of extinguishing those rights through treaties.

Specific claim. A claim made by a First Nation based on an alleged breach of fiduciary duty or responsibility on the part of Canada. Specific claims include, but are not restricted to, mismanagement of leases and reserves. Specific claims are negotiated outside of the treaty negotiation process.

Status Indian. *See* **Registered Indian**

Transboundary agreement. Treaties being negotiated with First Nations that claim rights and territory in both British Columbia and the Yukon.

Treaty. A negotiated agreement between a First Nation and government that defines the aboriginal rights of people of the nation.

Union of British Columbia Indian Chiefs (UBCIC). An umbrella organization representing the concerns of some First Nations in British Columbia. Most First Nations represented by the UBCIC are located in the southern interior of the province.

United Native Nations (UNN). An organization representing the interests of off-reserve Indians.

Selected Bibliography

In addition to the sources listed here, readers are encouraged to peruse *B.C. Studies*, which regularly publishes scholarly articles on First Nations people, cultures, and issues in British Columbia. Information on First Nations is also accessible through government web sites. The web site address of the provincial Ministry of Aboriginal Affairs is http://www.aaf.gov.bc.ca./aaf/. The web site address of Indian and Northern Affairs Canada is http://www.inac.gc.ca/index_e.html.

Adams, John W. 'Recent Ethnology on the Northwest Coast.' *Annual Review of Anthropology* 10 (1981): 361-92

Ames, Kenneth. 'The Northwest Coast: Complex Hunter-Gatherers, Ecology, and Social Evolution.' *Annual Review of Anthropology* 23 (1994): 209-25

Asch, Michael. *Home and Native Land: Aboriginal Rights and the Canadian Constitution*. Toronto: Methuen 1984

–, ed. *Aboriginal and Treaty Rights in Canada: Essays on Law, Equality, and Respect for Difference*. Vancouver: UBC Press 1997

Barman, Jean. *The West beyond the West: A History of British Columbia*. Revised edition. Toronto: University of Toronto Press 1996

Boldt, Menno. *Surviving as Indians: The Challenge of Self-Government*. Toronto: University of Toronto Press 1993

Bowering, George. *Bowering's B.C. A Swashbuckling History*. Toronto: Viking 1996

British Columbia. Ministry of Aboriginal Affairs. *A Guide to Aboriginal Organizations and Services in British Columbia*. Victoria: Ministry of Aboriginal Affairs 1997

Brody, Hugh. *Maps and Dreams: Indians and the British Columbia Frontier.* Vancouver: Douglas and McIntyre 1988

Canada. Indian and Northern Affairs Canada. *Schedule of Indian Bands, Reserves and Settlements.* Ottawa: Minister of Government Services 1992

Canada. Royal Commission on Aboriginal Peoples. *People to People, Nation to Nation: Highlights from the Report of the Royal Commission on Aboriginal Peoples.* Ottawa: Minister of Supply and Services 1996

Carlson, Roy L., ed. *Indian Art Traditions of the Northwest Coast.* Burnaby, BC: SFU Archaeology Press 1983

Carlson, Roy L., and Luke Dalla Bona, eds. *Early Human Occupation in British Columbia.* Vancouver: UBC Press 1996

Clark, Donald W. *Western Subarctic Prehistory.* Hull, QC: Canadian Museum of Civilization 1991

Coates, Ken S., and Robin Fisher. *Out of the Background: Readings on Canadian Native History.* 2nd ed. Toronto: Copp Clark 1996

Cole, Douglas. *Captured Heritage: The Scramble for Northwest Coast Artifacts.* Vancouver: UBC Press 1995

Comeau, Pauline, and Aldo Santin. *The First Canadians: A Profile of Canada's Native People Today.* 2nd ed. Toronto: Lorimer 1995

Coull, Cheryl. *A Traveller's Guide to Aboriginal B.C.* Vancouver: Whitecap Books 1996

Culhane, Dara. *The Pleasure of the Crown: Anthropology, Law and First Nations.* Vancouver: Talon Books 1998

Deloria, Vine. *Custer Died for Your Sins: An Indian Manifesto.* London: Collier-Macmillan 1969

Dickason, Olive P. *Canada's First Nations: A History of Founding Peoples from Earliest Times.* 2nd ed. Toronto: McClelland and Stewart 1997

Drucker, Philip. *Cultures of the North Pacific Coast.* New York: Harper and Row 1965

Duff, Wilson. *The Indian History of British Columbia*. Vol. 1, *The Impact of the White Man*. Anthropology in British Columbia Memoir no. 5. Victoria: British Columbia Provincial Museum 1965

Fisher, Robin. *Contact and Conflict: Indian-European Relations in British Columbia, 1774-1890*. 2nd ed. Vancouver: UBC Press 1992

Fladmark, Knut. *British Columbia Prehistory*. Ottawa: National Museums of Canada 1986

–. *Names and Dates: A Bibliography of British Columbia Archaeology*. Burnaby, BC: SFU Archaeology Press 1997

Francis, Daniel. *Copying People: Photographing British Columbia First Nations 1860-1940*. Calgary: Fifth House Publishers 1996

–. *The Imaginary Indian: The Image of the Indian in Canadian Culture*. Vancouver: Arsenal Pulp Press 1992

Frideres, James S. *Native People in Canada: Contemporary Conflicts*. 5th ed. Toronto: Prentice-Hall 1998

Furniss, Elizabeth. *Victims of Benevolence: The Dark Legacy of the Williams Lake Residential School*. Vancouver: Arsenal 1995

Gadacz, René. Selected articles on BC First Nations ethnography, including multimedia. *Canadian and World Encyclopedia on CD-Rom*. Toronto: McClelland and Stewart 1998

Glavin, Terry. *A Death Feast in Dimlahamid*. Vancouver: New Star Books 1990

Haig-Brown, Celia. *Resistance and Renewal: Surviving the Indian Residential School*. Vancouver: Tillacum 1988

Hall, Lizette. *The Carrier, My People*. Quesnel, BC: L. Hall 1992

Halpin, Marjorie M. *Totem Poles: An Illustrated Guide*. Vancouver: UBC Press and the UBC Museum of Anthropology 1981

Harris, Cole. *The Resettlement of British Columbia: Essays on Colonialism and Geographical Change*. Vancouver: UBC Press 1997

Hayden, Brian. *The Pithouses of Keatley Creek: Complex Hunter-Gatherers of the Northwest Plateau.* Toronto: Harcourt Brace 1997

–, ed. *A Complex Culture of the British Columbia Plateau: Stl'atl'imx Resource Use.* Vancouver: UBC Press 1992

Hedican, Edward J. *Applied Anthropology in Canada: Understanding Aboriginal Issues.* Toronto: University of Toronto Press 1995

Helm, June, ed. *Handbook of North American Indians.* Vol. 6, *Subarctic.* Washington: Smithsonian Institution 1981

Holm, Bill. *Northwest Coast Indian Art: An Analysis of Form.* Vancouver: Douglas and McIntyre 1965

Jensen, Doreen, and Cheryl Brooks, eds. *In Celebration of Our Survival: The First Nations of British Columbia.* Vancouver: UBC Press 1991

Johnston, Hugh J.M., ed. *The Pacific Province: A History of British Columbia.* Vancouver: Douglas and McIntyre 1996

Kehoe, Alice B. *North American Indians: A Comprehensive Account.* 2nd ed. Toronto: Prentice-Hall 1992

Kennedy, Dorothy, and Randy Bouchard. *Sliammon Life, Sliammon Lands.* Vancouver: Talon Books 1983

Kew, J.E. Michael. 'Anthropology and First Nations in B.C.' *B.C. Studies* 100 (1994): 78-105

Kramer, Pat. *Native Sites in Western Canada.* Canmore, AB: Altitude 1994

McKee, Christopher. *Treaty Talks in British Columbia: Negotiating a Mutually Beneficial Future.* Vancouver: UBC Press 1996

McMillan, Alan D. *Native Peoples and Cultures of Canada: An Anthropological Overview.* 2nd ed. Vancouver: Douglas and McIntyre 1995

Mathias, Chief Joe, and Gary R. Yabsley. 'Conspiracy of Legislation: The Suppression of Indian Rights in Canada.' *B.C. Studies* 89 (1991): 34-45

Matson, R.G., and Gary Coupland. *Prehistory of the Northwest Coast.* New York: Academic Press 1994

Maud, Ralph. *A Guide to B.C. Indian Myth and Legend.* Vancouver: Talon Books 1982

–, ed. *The Salish People: The Local Contributions of Charles Hill-Tout.* Vols. 1-4. Vancouver: Talon Books 1978

Miller, J.R. *Shingwauk's Vision: A History of Native Residential Schools.* Toronto: University of Toronto Press 1996

Morrison, R. Bruce, and C. Roderick Wilson, eds. *Native Peoples: The Canadian Experience.* 2nd ed. Toronto: McClelland and Stewart 1995

Newell, Dianne. *Tangled Webs of History: Indians and the Law in Canada's Pacific Coast Fisheries.* Toronto: University of Toronto Press 1993

Nicholas, George P., and Thomas D. Andrews, eds. *At a Crossroads: Archaeology and First Peoples in Canada.* Burnaby, BC: SFU Archaeology Press 1997

Nisga'a Tribal Council. *Nisga'a: People of the Nass River.* Vancouver: Douglas and McIntyre and Nisga'a Tribal Council 1993

Purich, Donald. *Our Land: Native Rights in Canada.* Toronto: Lorimer 1986

Ray, Arthur J. *I Have Lived Here since the World Began: An Illustrated History of Canada's Native People.* Toronto: Lester Publishing and Key Porter Books 1996

Richards, Thomas H., and Michael K. Rousseau. *Late Prehistoric Cultural Horizons on the Canadian Plateau.* Burnaby, BC: SFU Archaeology Press 1987

Rosman, Abraham, and Paula G. Rubel. *Feasting with Mine Enemy: Rank and Exchange among Northwest Coast Societies.* Prospect Heights, IL: Waveland 1986

Smart, Stephen B., and Michael Coyle, eds. *Aboriginal Issues Today: A Legal and Business Guide.* North Vancouver: Self-Counsel Press 1997

Smith, Melvin H. *Our Home or Native Land? What Government's Aboriginal Policy is Doing to Canada.* Victoria: Crown Western 1995

Stephenson, Peter H., Susan J. Elliot, Leslie T. Foster, and Jill Harris, eds. *A Persistent Spirit: Towards Understanding Aboriginal Health in British Columbia.* Canadian Western Geographical Series Vol. 31. Victoria: University of Victoria 1995

Stewart, Hilary. *Looking at Indian Art of the Northwest Coast.* Vancouver: Douglas and McIntyre 1979

Suttles, Wayne. *Coast Salish Essays.* Vancouver: Talon Books 1987

–, ed. *Handbook of North American Indians.* Vol. 7, *Northwest Coast.* Washington: Smithsonian Institution 1990

Teit, James. *The Lillooet Indians.* New York: American Museum of Natural History 1906

–. *The Shuswap.* New York: American Museum of Natural History 1909

–. *The Thompson Indians.* New York: American Museum of Natural History 1900 *

Tennant, Paul. *Aboriginal Peoples and Politics: The Indian Land Question in British Columbia, 1849-1989.* Vancouver: UBC Press 1990

Turner, Nancy. *Food Plants of Coastal First Peoples.* Vancouver: UBC Press 1996

–. *Food Plants of Interior First Peoples.* Vancouver: UBC Press 1997

Webster, Gloria Cranmer. 'From Colonization to Repatriation.' In *Indigena: Contemporary Native Perspectives,* edited by Gerald McMaster and Lee-Ann Martin, 25-37. Vancouver: Douglas and McIntyre 1992

Wickwire, Wendy. 'Ethnography and Archaeology as Ideology: The Case Study of the Stein River Valley.' *B.C. Studies* 91-2 (1991-2): 51-78

Set in Giovanni Book by Artegraphica Design Co.

Printed and bound in Canada by Friesens

Cartographer: Eric Leinberger

Copy editor: Camilla Jenkins

Designer: Irma Rodriguez

Proofreader: Gail Copeland